CICERO'S SOMNIUM SCIPIONIS

The Dream of Scipio

Prepared by Sally Davis and Gilbert Lawall

LONGMAN

Longman, 10 Bank Street, White Plains, N.Y. 10606

Associated companies:
Longman Group Ltd., London
Longman Cheshire Pty., Melbourne
Longman Paul Pty., Auckland
Copp Clark Pitman, Toronto
Pitman Publishing Inc., New York

Authors: **Sally Davis**, Wakefield High School,
Arlington, Virginia
Professor Gilbert Lawall, University of Massachusetts,
Amherst, Massachusetts
Series Editor: **Professor Gilbert Lawall**
Consultants: **Jane Harriman Hall**, Mary Washington College,
Fredericksburg, Virginia
Richard A. LaFleur, University of Georgia,
Athens, Georgia
Robert E. Morse, Saint Andrew's School,
Boca Raton, Florida

Executive editor: Lyn McLean
Production editor: Elsa van Bergen
Text and cover designer: Gayle Jaeger
Production supervisor: Judith Stern

ISBN 0-582-36751-4

13 14 - CRS - 05

CONTENTS

ACKNOWLEDGMENTS

The authors wish to thank Professor Cynthia King of Wright State University for numerous helpful suggestions offered as a result of her teaching of the "Somnium Scipionis" from this text in her Latin class at Wright State. The authors also wish to acknowledge their debt to the commentaries on the "Somnium" that are listed in the Bibliography in the teacher's handbook. Much has been gleaned from their pages and incorporated into the present edition.

INTRODUCTION

CICERO

Marcus Tullius Cicero was born at Arpinum in 106 B.C. of a well-to-do family of some local distinction. Both he and his brother Quintus showed such aptitude for learning that their father brought them to Rome to study rhetoric, philosophy, and law. When Cicero was 26, he began pleading causes in the Senate, and from the beginning of his career it was apparent that he possessed outstanding ability in oratory. He served as quaestor (75 B.C.), curule aedile (69 B.C.), praetor (66 B.C.), and finally consul (63 B.C.).

During the second half of his consulship, Cicero distinguished himself by suppressing the anarchist conspiracy of the desperate and unscrupulous Catiline and his band of associates. This was the greatest feat of his political leadership. He refused to join the so-called First Triumvirate (60 B.C.), a coalition of Pompey, Crassus, and Caesar, and was forced to leave Rome for a year in exile (58 B.C.). He returned in 57 B.C. but found the political situation in Rome increasingly uncomfortable. When the triumvirate reaffirmed its power at the conference of Luca in 56 B.C., Cicero was put in such a compromising situation that he largely retired from public life and began writing works on oratory (*De oratore*) and philosophy (*De republica*). When civil war threatened (49 B.C.), he vacillated between Caesar and Pompey but finally sided with Pompey, who was defeated by Caesar at the battle of Pharsalus (48 B.C.). During Caesar's dictatorship, Cicero quietly returned to his writing. After the assassination of Caesar (44 B.C.), Cicero again came into political prominence, this time risking the antipathy and vengeance of Antony. He wrote fourteen speeches, called the *Philippics*, of bitter invective against Antony's tyrannical efforts to suppress liberty. After the Second Triumvirate was formed, Cicero was murdered by Antony's agents in 43 B.C., and his head and hands were displayed on the rostra in the Forum.

In addition to his forensic orations, Cicero left a voluminous correspondence and numerous philosophical and literary writings. Quintilian (first century A.D.) regarded Cicero as the greatest of Roman writers, and it is generally accepted that in his writing he brought Latin prose to its perfection, whereby it became the basis of literary expression in the languages of modern Europe.

THE *DE REPUBLICA*

Cicero's idea of writing a treatise on government may have originated when he read Plato's book on the ideal state, the *Republic*. Cicero began writing his *De republica* in 54 B.C. during his forcible exclusion from politics at Rome, and he published it in 51 B.C. He wrote his treatise in the form of a dialogue, as Plato had, and he dealt with many of the same topics: the three basic forms of government, the ideal statesman, the nature of justice, and the best education for the good citizen. Cicero's *De republica*, however, was no mere translation of Plato's work but a highly original treatment of these vital questions. It consisted of six books, two for each day of a three-day holiday conversation. The scene is set carefully and vividly. The time is April of the year 129 B.C., and all of Rome is celebrating the Latin Holidays. Seven of Rome's outstanding noblemen have come to the country villa of Scipio the Younger, an eminent and experienced statesman, to spend the three days in profitable discussion of the philosophy of government. As each one arrives, he is greeted warmly by Scipio and the others; then the whole group walks through the portico of Scipio's garden, and finally they recline on couches in the crisp April air on the sunniest part of the lawn. The atmosphere of the dialogue is one of deep friendship, of nobility and intimacy, and of profound concern and philosophical inquiry. The principal speakers are Scipio and Laelius. Of the six books that Cicero wrote, we have the greater part of the first three, fragments of the next three, and the entire concluding passage on the dream of Scipio.

At the beginning of the work as the guests are still arriving, there is discussion of a recent sighting of a second sun that had been reported to the Senate. The discussion of this unusual sight leads to reminiscences of similar phenomena and the attempts of astronomers to explain them, but the discussion quickly passes to more pressing concerns of disturbances not in the heavens but in the Roman state. The controversy over the agrarian reforms of Tiberius Gracchus, tribune of the plebs, who was slain in 133 B.C. by a band of senators, has split the state into two opposing factions. Concern over this open rift in the Roman state leads to the question of what is the best form of government. Scipio sets forth the three typical forms of government— monarchy, aristocracy, and democracy—with the degenerative counterparts of each. He then proposes that the ideal form of government is a combination of the three good forms. He offers the Roman Republic as the embodiment of this composite and uses it throughout the rest of the work as an illustration of the ideal. The virtue of the composite state is stability; Cicero's ideal is not an equilibrium of forces but a concord like the harmony of music.

In contrast to the theoretical approach that Plato employed, Cicero begins empirically with the Roman constitution as it developed in the course of history. Its strength and solidarity actually derive from the fact that it evolved over a long period of time. Yet if the early Roman Republic was the ideal state and Scipio the ideal Roman statesman, what is Cicero saying about the political situation of his own time? In the past, Scipio protected and preserved Roman tradition, did not seek individual glory for himself, and died (possibly at the hands of his political enemies) at the height of his opposition to the reform legislation of the Gracchi, which many in the Senate saw as threatening the constitution and the stability of the state. In Cicero's own time the Roman state was again being divided against itself, most notably through the actions of Caesar and Pompey. The message that comes through clearly is Cicero's exhortation that it is each citizen's highest duty to serve his country and devote his best efforts to this pursuit rather than to the pursuit of individual glory, fame, and power.

While Cicero's writing and publication of the *De republica* do not seem to have had any restraining influence on Caesar or Pompey, the emphasis on the importance of a strong guiding hand at the tiller of government may have had a real influence on the theory and practice of the early Principate, which followed the civil wars initiated by Caesar and Pompey. If this was indeed the case, there is a degree of irony in the fact that Octavian, who was to become the first **princeps** and the future Augustus, was one of those who consented to Cicero's proscription and his murder by agents of Antony.

THE "DREAM OF SCIPIO" OR "SOMNIUM SCIPIONIS"

The impressive form and the grand scope of the concluding section of the *De republica*, the "Dream of Scipio" or "Somnium Scipionis," have attracted readers, scholars, and poets of all ages. The story is modeled on the myth of Er at the end of the tenth and last book of Plato's *Republic*, and, like the myth of Er, it deals with the life of the soul after death. Scipio is visited in his dream by his famous ancestor, Scipio the Elder, who foretells the future. The picture of the two Scipios standing "in a lofty place bathed in clear starlight" and gazing down first on the entire universe and finally onto the tiny planet earth is particularly appealing in these days of space exploration.

Toward the end of the third day of the Holidays Scipio tells the group about his dream. He asks everyone to be silent and begs their indulgence so that he may relate to them the dream that he had many years before— twenty, to be exact. The dream has been very much on his mind during the entire three days, for in it he was told that all the threads of his life would come together and be tied off when he had reached the fateful fifty-sixth year of his life. He has now reached this age. The revelation of the dream to the participants of the dialogue, however, is not a digression from the discussion of the ideal state but rather the perfect finishing touch. It marks a critical turning point in the development of government and political activity in the Roman Republic, and it looks forward to the gathering of loyal Roman states- men who created and protected the Republic—a gathering in their everlast- ing home in the realm of the fiery stars.

SCIPIO THE ELDER

Publius Cornelius Scipio Africanus Major (the Elder) (236–183 B.C.) is well- known in Roman history for his victory over Hannibal at Zama in 202 B.C., which brought the Second Punic War to an end. He is first mentioned at the battle of Ticinus, where he saved his father's life (218 B.C.). He fought as a military tribune at Cannae (216 B.C.) and was one of the few Roman officers to survive that battle. When he was only 25 years of age, he was appointed to the command of the army in Spain. Here he took Carthago Nova, and during the next three years he drove the Carthaginians back to Africa. He was elected consul for the year 205 B.C., and in 204 B.C. he obtained an army and crossed to Africa. Hannibal was recalled from Italy and suffered his final defeat at Zama at the hands of Scipio. In 201 B.C. Scipio returned to Rome, where he celebrated his triumph and received the cognomen Africanus. He died in retirement on his estate at Liternum in Campania in 183 B.C.

SCIPIO THE YOUNGER

Publius Cornelius Scipio Aemilianus, known as Scipio Africanus Minor (the Younger), was born ca. 185 B.C., the son of Lucius Aemilius Paulus, the conqueror of Macedonia. Upon the death of his father, Scipio was adopted by P. Scipio, the son of Scipio Africanus Major. The younger Scipio served with great distinction as military tribune in Spain (151 B.C.), and he went to Africa as military tribune in 149 B.C. When the Third Punic War threatened disaster, he was elected consul, although he was under age and only a candidate for the aedileship. He successfully besieged Carthage and destroyed it in 146 B.C. despite the heroic resistance of the defenders; in 142 B.C. he served as censor, and in 134 B.C. he was again chosen consul, to bring the war against Numantia in Spain to an end. When he returned to Rome, he allied himself with the aristocratic party (the **Optimātēs**) even though his brothers-in-law, the Gracchi, were leaders of the popular party (the **Populārēs**). He could not accept the policies of the latter, and he bitterly opposed their legislation for redistribution of public lands. He was found dead in 129 B.C., and in the gossip of the time the Gracchan faction was implicated in his death.

Scipio loved literature and philosophy, law and government; he attracted the most famous Greek and Latin intellectuals and literati of his time (later known as the Scipionic Circle). Scipio represented what Cicero thought of as the best in Roman character at a historical moment that came to be regarded as a great turning point in the development of the Roman Republic. Cicero regarded Scipio the Younger as the greatest of the Romans.

THE GRACCHI

Tiberius Sempronius Gracchus was born in 168 B.C., the son of Tiberius Sempronius Gracchus and Cornelia (daughter of Scipio Africanus Major), famous for her virtue and accomplishments. As Tiberius grew up, his sympathy was roused by the distressed condition of Italy, large tracts of which were completely deserted while the huge estates of the wealthy few were cultivated only by slave labor. With the intention of halting the gradual extinction of the peasant farmers, from whom the legions were recruited, Tiberius Gracchus in 133 B.C. proposed a bill before the Senate that limited the amount of public land anyone could own. The proposal met with fierce opposition from the wealthy, but nevertheless it was passed and a commission was appointed to carry out its provisions. When Tiberius sought reelection for the following year, however, he was killed by a group of senators led by P. Cornelius Scipio Nasica Serapio. Tiberius' brother Gaius carried on his work, despite the strong opposition of Scipio the Younger, and enacted a number of far-reaching agrarian, military, and franchise reforms. Reaction hardened, and in 121 B.C. a **senātūs cōnsultum ultimum** was passed against him. When Gaius and his supporters were attacked, he ordered a faithful slave to kill him. Substantial ideological and political differences separated the Gracchi from men like Scipio Nasica and Scipio the Younger, and these differences were serious enough, despite the familial relationship through Cornelia, to result in murder.

THE MANUSCRIPT TRADITION

Although the account of the dream of Scipio was written as the concluding episode of the *De republica*, the two have separate and distinct manuscript traditions. Except for the account of the dream of Scipio, the *De republica* was known in the later Middle Ages and until the nineteenth century only from scattered short quotations in other works or authors. In 1820 Cardinal Angelo Mai, the prefect of the Vatican Library, made the spectacular discovery of a manuscript of the fifth or sixth century A.D., which had originally contained Cicero's *De republica*. Cicero's work had been partially erased from the parchment, and a scribe had used the same parchment to copy St. Augustine's commentary on the Psalms. Enough of Cicero's *De republica* was still visible beneath the commentary on the Psalms to allow scholars to decipher about one-third of the entire text.

The account of the dream of Scipio survived intact throughout the Middle Ages. This small portion of the *De republica* attracted widespread attention in antiquity and the Middle Ages because of its visionary quality and its account of the afterlife of the soul, which appealed to pagans and Christians alike. In the early fifth century A.D. a Roman grammarian by the name of Ambrosius Macrobius wrote an elaborate commentary on Scipio's dream, to which he appended the text of this portion of the *De republica*. Macrobius' commentary deals mainly with the significance of dreams, the theory of perfect numbers, and the immortality of the soul. A pupil of St. Augustine, a certain Favonius Eulogius, wrote a similar work. Both of these, but especially the work of Macrobius, served to ensure the survival of the dream of Scipio throughout the Middle Ages until the eleventh century, when it was copied at Paris and at Hamburg in manuscripts which we still possess. Cicero's account of the dream of Scipio as preserved by Macrobius served as one of the main vehicles of the transmission of Platonic philosophy to Christian Europe; both Dante and Chaucer incorporated it in their work. Something of the seminal significance of the "Dream of Scipio" is suggested by the concluding words of Macrobius' commentary:

Vērē igitur prōnūntiandum est nihil hōc opere perfectius, quō ūniversa philosophiae continētur integritās.

Truly then it must be declared that nothing is more perfect than this work, in which is contained the sum total of philosophy.

—MACROBIUS, II.17.17

SOMNIUM
SCIPIONIS

1 **Cum . . . vēnissem**: what kind of a **cum** clause is this? What is the tense of the subjunctive? Why is this tense used here?

M'. Mānīliō cōnsulī: "under the consul Manius Manilius" (149 B.C.), dative with **tribūnus** (2) showing the relationship of the tribune to the consul.   **ad**: = **apud.**

2 **tribūnus . . . mīlitum**: "tribune of the soldiers" (an army officer, six to each legion, who commanded in turn, each two months at a time; see *The Oxford Classical Dictionary*, "**Tribuni Militum**," pp. 1091–1092). The younger Scipio, at 35 years of age, had already distinguished himself militarily in Macedonia and Spain; he has now been sent to Africa to aid Manilius at the outbreak of the Third Punic War.

ut scītis: parenthetical, addressed to the others present at the three-day-long discussion of the ideal state, and suggesting a conversational style (cf. our "you know").

potior, potius, preferable, more important.

Masinissa, -ae (*m*), king of Numidia. Originally an ally of the Carthaginians, Masinissa later joined the elder Scipio in the final stages of the Second Punic War. He fought in the battle of Zama (202 B.C.), where Hannibal was finally defeated. After this, he ruled all of Numidia as an ally of Rome for fifty years; when the younger Scipio arrived in Africa, Masinissa was in his ninetieth and last year (he died in 148 B.C.).

3 **conveniō, convenīre** (4), **convēnī, conventum,** to visit. Here used with **ut** in a substantive clause of purpose. What tense of the subjunctive is **convenīrem**? Why is this tense used?

Ad quem (4): linking **quī** = **Et ad eum**; Latin frequently uses a relative at the beginning of a sentence where English prefers a personal pronoun.

4 ***complector, complectī** (3), **complexus sum,** to embrace. Is the perfect participle of a deponent verb active or passive in meaning?

conlacrimāvit: the prefix adds emphasis.

aliquantō, somewhat, a little. Here modifying the adverb ***post**, afterward.

5 **suspiciō, suspicere** (3), **suspexī, suspectum,** to look up. ***caelum, -ī** (*n*), sky, heavens.

grātēs (*f pl*), thanks. **grātēs agere**, to thank.

6 **caelitēs, caelitum** (*m/f pl*), the inhabitants of heaven (**caelum**), the gods. Poetic word; here referring to the moon, planets, and stars, thought of as divine bodies, and here capitalized, indicating personification.

antequam, before.   ***migrō** (1), to depart. & *not*

7 **tēctum, -ī** (*n*), roof, building. (frequently in the plural for a single building).

P. Cornēlium Scīpiōnem: note that this name was shared by the elder and the younger Scipio; memories of the elder Scipio rejuvenate Masinissa by bringing back the remote past.

recreō (1), to make anew, refresh, rejuvenate.

8 **itaque**, and so, therefore. Masinissa means that since he is rejuvenated by merely thinking of the name of Scipio, that name will never fade from his memory.

*discēdō, discēdere (3), **discessī, discessum,** to go away, depart.

illīus . . . virī (9): i.e., Scipio Africanus Major.   **invictus, -a, -um**, unconquerable.

9 **suō**: = **eius.**

10 **percontor, percontārī** (1), **percontātus sum**, to ask, question. The verb agrees in person with the closer subject, **ille**, but is meant to be understood with **ego** as well. This usage is termed *syllepsis.*

verbum, -ī (*n*), word.   **ultrō**, on the other side.   **citrō**, on this side.   **ultrō citrōque**, on this side and on that, on both sides.

nōbīs: either dative of agent ("by us") or dative of reference ("our whole day").

The younger Scipio tells how upon arriving in Africa he met King Masinissa of Numidia.

1 **IX.** Cum in Āfricam vēnissem M'. Mānīliō cōnsulī ad quārtam legiōnem
2 tribūnus, ut scītis, mīlitum, nihil mihi fuit potius quam ut Masinissam
3 convenīrem, rēgem familiae nostrae iūstīs dē causīs amīcissimum. Ad
4 quem ut vēnī, complexus mē senex conlacrimāvit aliquantōque post
5 suspexit ad caelum et, "Grātēs," inquit, "tibi agō, summe Sōl, vōbīsque,
6 reliquī Caelitēs, quod, antequam ex hāc vītā migrō, cōnspiciō in meō
7 rēgnō et hīs tēctīs P. Cornēlium Scīpiōnem, cuius ego nōmine recreor ipsō;
8 itaque numquam ex animō meō discēdit illīus optimī atque invictissimī
9 virī memoria." Deinde ego illum dē suō rēgnō, ille mē dē nostrā rē pūblicā
10 percontātus est, multīsque verbīs ultrō citrōque habitīs ille nōbīs est
11 cōnsumptus diēs.

1. Why had Scipio come to Africa? (1–2)
2. What did Scipio especially want to do when he arrived? Why? (2–3)
3. How did Masinissa show his feelings when Scipio came to him? (3–4)
4. Why was Masinissa glad to see the younger Scipio? (5–9)
5. What were Masinissa's feelings about the elder Scipio? (8–9)
6. How did Masinissa and Scipio spend the day? (9–11)

This map shows the entire Mediterranean area as it was at the time when Scipio the Younger described his dream.

12 **Post**: adverb here.

apparātus, -ūs (*m*), preparation, splendor, magnificence (here referring to a lavish banquet).

acceptī: "entertained."

*sermō, sermōnis (*m*), conversation. **in multam noctem**: "late into the night."

13 **prōdūcō, prōdūcere** (3), **prōdūxī, prōductum**, to draw out, extend.

cum, (here) while, and during this time. What kind of a **cum** clause is this?

loquerētur: what tense of the subjunctive is this, and why is this tense used here?

14 **factum, -ī** (*n*), deed, achievement.

dictum, -ī (*n*), word, saying.

*meminī, meminisse, to remember, recall, mention. This verb has only tense forms that are based on the perfect stem; the perfect tense has present meanings, and the pluperfect tense has imperfect meanings. Accordingly, the pluperfect subjunctive is here used where one would expect the imperfect subjunctive.

cubō, cubāre (1), **cubuī, cubitum**, to lie down, sleep. The supine in the accusative expresses purpose after verbs of motion.

15 **mē**: object of **complexus est** (16).

fessus, -a, -um, tired. Here with the force of a causal clause.

quī, (here) since, because (+ subjunctive).

*vigilō (1), to stay awake, be awake. **vigilāssem**: = **vigilāvissem**; what tense of the subjunctive is this, and why is this tense used here?

16 **artus, -a, -um**, close, confined, tight, (of sleep) sound, deep.

*soleō, solēre (2), **solitus sum**, to be accustomed.

*somnus, -ī (*m*), sleep.

mihi: construe with **Āfricānus sē ostendit** below (19).

*equidem, indeed.

ex hōc (17) **quod**: "as a result of what."

17 **ut . . . pariant** (18): substantive clause of result after the verb **fit**, "it usually happens that. . . ."

cōgitātiō, cōgitātiōnis (*f*), thought.

18 ***pariō, parere** (3), **peperī, partum**, to bring forth, give birth to, bring about, produce.

pariant aliquid: i.e., dreams reproduce what we were thinking about or experiencing before going to sleep.

tāle quāle: "such as."

Ennius: Ennius (239–169 B.C., regarded by the Romans as the father of their poetry) at the beginning of his epic poem on the history of Rome, the *Annales*, wrote of a dream in which the Greek epic poet Homer appeared to him and explained that his soul had migrated into Ennius' body.

dē quō . . . solēbat (19): "about whom (i.e., Homer) he used to. . . ."

19 **vidēlicet** (*adv.*), it is easy to see, clearly, evidently, of course.

20 **imāgō, imāginis** (*f*), image, statue, bust, picture. Roman aristocrats decorated the **ātria** of their houses with waxen images or death masks of their ancestors. The younger Scipio could not have remembered his grandfather himself, who died (184/183 B.C.) when the younger Scipio was only one or two years old (born 185/184 B.C.).

20 ***nōtus, -a, -um**, known.

quem: linking **quī**.

21 **agnōscō, agnōscere** (3), **agnōvī, agnitum**, to recognize.

cohorrēscō, cohorrēscere (3), **cohorruī**, to shudder, quiver with fear.

Ades: imperative of **adsum**. **Ades . . . animō**: "Be present in mind," "Pay attention," "Gather your courage."

omittō, omittere (3), **omīsī, omissum**, to abandon, cease.

22 **quae**: supply **haec**, "the following," as antecedent.

8

Scipio and Masinissa reminisced until late at night. Upon going to bed, Scipio had a dream about his adoptive grandfather.

12 **X.** Post autem apparātū rēgiō acceptī, sermōnem in multam noctem
13 prōdūximus, cum senex nihil nisi dē Āfricānō loquerētur omniaque eius
14 nōn facta sōlum sed etiam dicta meminisset. Deinde ut cubitum
15 discessimus, mē et dē viā fessum, et quī ad multam noctem vigilāssem,
16 artior quam solēbat somnus complexus est. Hīc mihi (crēdō equidem ex
17 hōc quod erāmus locūtī; fit enim ferē ut cōgitātiōnēs sermōnēsque nostrī
18 pariant aliquid in somnō tāle quāle dē Homērō scrībit Ennius, dē quō
19 vidēlicet saepissimē vigilāns solēbat cōgitāre et loquī) Āfricānus sē ostendit
20 eā fōrmā quae mihi ex imāgine eius quam ex ipsō erat nōtior; quem ubi
21 agnōvī, equidem cohorruī; sed ille, "Ades," inquit, "animō et omitte
22 timōrem, Scīpiō, et quae dīcam memoriae trāde.

1. How did the conversation between Masinissa and Scipio after dinner differ from their talk earlier in the day? (12–14)
2. For what two reasons was Scipio's sleep deeper than usual? (15)
3. What experience of Ennius does the younger Scipio recall? (18–19)
4. How did the younger Scipio recognize his adoptive grandfather in the dream? (19–21)
5. How did he react to the appearance of his adoptive grandfather? (21)
6. What does his adoptive grandfather order him to do? (21–22)

Scipio Africanus the Elder

9

23 **per mē**: Carthage was defeated and forced into accepting harsh peace terms by the elder Africanus in 202 B.C. after his victory at Zama.

24 **renovō** (1), to renew.

pristinus, -a, -um, former, preceding, past. The **pristina bella** are the First and Second Punic Wars (see *The Oxford Classical Dictionary*, "Punic Wars," pp. 900-901).

quiēscō, quiēscere (3), **quiēvī, quiētum**, to be quiet, be at peace.

***autem**, (here) and in fact, and indeed (often used with this meaning in a parenthesis).

25 **dē**: with **locō**, which is modified by five adjectives in between.

excelsus, -a, -um, elevated, lofty, high. ***plēnus, -a, -um** (+ *gen.*), full (of).

***stella, -ae** (*f*), star. **illustris, -is, -e**, light, bright, lustrous. **clārus, -a, -um**, bright.

26 **Ad quam . . . oppugnandam**: "To attack it," gerundive with **ad** to express purpose.

paene mīles: "almost a (mere) soldier." Young men of senatorial or equestrian rank were chosen as military tribunes. Here the elder Scipio refers to the office as a lowly one in contrast to the consulship to which the younger Scipio will rise in two years' time.

biennium, -ī (*n*), period of two years.

27 **ēvertō, ēvertere** (3), **ēvertī, ēversum**, to overturn, overthrow, destroy. **cōnsul ēvertēs**: not exactly true; Scipio was consul in 147 B.C. and proconsul the following year (146), in which he captured and destroyed Carthage and celebrated a triumph.

cognōmen, cognōminis (*n*), name added to the **nōmen**. Here: "Africanus Minor."

partum: "earned," from **pariō, parere** (3), **peperī, partum**, to bring forth, produce.

adhūc, until now.

28 **ā nōbīs**: "from me." **hērēditārius, -a, -um**, inherited.

Cum . . . .: the **cum** clause contains four verbs in the future perfect, and the main clause contains three verbs in the future.

triumphus, -ī (*m*), triumphal entrance of a general into Rome after having obtained an important victory. **triumphum ēgeris** (29): "you will celebrate your triumph." See *The Oxford Classical Dictionary*, "Triumph," p. 1095, for a description of the triumphal procession.

29 **cēnsor, cēnsōris** (*m*), censor. The younger Scipio held this office in 142 B.C. For the office of the censorship, see *The Oxford Classical Dictionary*, "Censor," p. 219. This office was the culmination of the **cursus honōrum** (see *The Oxford Classical Dictionary*, "Cursus Honorum," p. 303).

obeō, obīre (*irreg.*), **obīvī** or **obiī, obitum**, to go to, pass through, visit.

lēgātus, -ī (*m*), ambassador. About 140 B.C., Scipio was sent out as ambassador to settle the affairs of Greece and the Near East. (Cicero in the *Academica*, II.5, places this mission as ambassador before Scipio's censorship instead of after it as here.)

30 **dēligēre**: = **dēligēris** (2nd person singular, future passive of **dēligō, dēligere**, to choose).

iterum (*adv.*), again.

absēns: the younger Scipio was elected consul again in 134 B.C. even though he was not in Rome to stand as a candidate; this is represented as an exceptional honor.

bellum . . . maximum: the war in Spain, brought to a turning point by Scipio's capture of Numantia after a siege of fifteen months (133 B.C.).

31 **excindō, excindere** (3), **excidī, excissum**, to tear out, destroy.

currus, -ūs (*m*), chariot, triumphal chariot. The reference is to Scipio's triumph in 132 B.C. after the Numantine war, which had been brought to an end the previous year.

invehō, invehere (3), **invexī, invectum**, to carry into a place.

offendō, offendere (3), **offendī, offēnsum**, to hit against, hit upon, meet with, find.

32 **perturbātus, -a, -um**, troubled, disturbed.

nepōs, nepōtis (*m*), grandson. The reference is to Tiberius Gracchus, son of Cornelia (daughter of the elder Scipio) and tribune in 133 B.C. His proposals for land reform were oppposed by the Senate, and he was killed in a riot (provoked by the senatorial faction) in 133 B.C. after passage of his legislation in the popular assembly. The younger Scipio, upon his return from the Numantine war in 132 B.C., added to this disturbed state of affairs in Rome by championing the senatorial resistance to the Gracchan reforms.

10

Scipio Africanus Major predicts the brilliant political and military success that will come to his nephew.

23 **XI.** "Vidēsne illam urbem, quae pārēre populō Rōmānō coācta per mē
24 renovat pristina bella nec potest quiēscere?" (Ostendēbat autem
25 Karthāginem dē excelsō et plēnō stellārum, illustrī et clārō quōdam locō.)
26 "Ad quam tū oppugnandam nunc venīs paene mīles. Hanc hōc bienniō
27 cōnsul ēvertēs, eritque cognōmen id tibi per tē partum, quod habēs adhūc
28 ā nōbīs hērēditārium. Cum autem Karthāginem dēlēveris, triumphum
29 ēgeris cēnsorque fueris et obieris lēgātus Aegyptum, Syriam, Asiam,
30 Graeciam, dēligēre iterum cōnsul absēns bellumque maximum cōnficiēs,
31 Numantiam excindēs. Sed cum eris currū in Capitōlium invectus, offendēs
32 rem pūblicam cōnsiliīs perturbātam nepōtis meī.

1. **What did the elder Scipio do to Carthage, and what is Carthage doing now?** (23–24)
2. **From what vantage point are the younger Scipio and his adoptive grandfather looking at Carthage?** (24–25)
3. **What offices will the younger Scipio hold?** (27–30)
4. **What cities will he destroy?** (28–31)
5. **What honors will he receive?** (27–31)
6. **In what condition will he find Rome after his return from Spain?** (31–32)
7. **Upon whom does the elder Scipio place blame for this state of affairs?** (32)

REM PŪBLICAM CŌNSILIĪS PERTURBĀTAM

The nobles began to abuse their position and the people their liberty, and every man for himself robbed, pillaged, and plundered. Thus the community was split into two parties, and between these the state was torn to pieces.

—SALLUST, *Bellum Iugurthinum* XLI.5, translated by J. C. Rolfe

The stability of the community was shattered by Tiberius Gracchus.

—CICERO, *De haruspicum responsis* XIX.41, translated by N. H. Watts

Tiberius Gracchus proposed an agrarian law. The law was acceptable to the People: the fortunes of the poorer classes seemed likely to be established. The Optimates opposed it, because they saw in it an incentive to dissension, and also thought that the State would be stripped of its champions by the eviction of the rich from their long-established tenancies.

—CICERO, *Pro Sestio* XLVIII.103, translated by R. Gardner

*Scipio Africanus the Younger, from a bust at the Museo
Nazionale, Naples.*

Some Cornelii, Aemilii, and Sempronii Gracchi

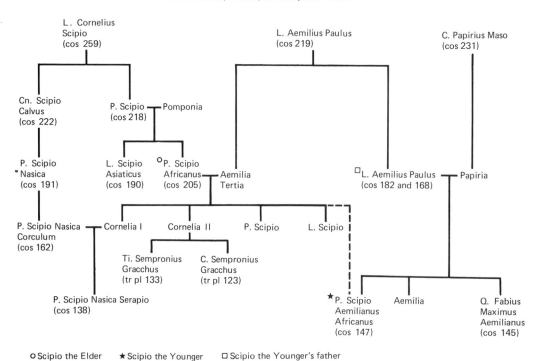

He [Tiberius Gracchus] was a man of otherwise blameless life, of brilliant intellect, of upright intentions, and, in a word, endowed with the highest virtues of which a man is capable when favored by nature and by training. In the consulship of Publius Mucius Scaevola and Lucius Calpurnius . . . , he split with the party of the nobles, promised the citizenship to all Italy, and at the same time, by proposing agrarian laws which all immediately desired to see in operation, turned the state topsy turvy, and brought it into a position of critical and extreme danger. He abrogated the power of his colleague Octavius, who defended the interests of the state, and appointed a commission of three to assign lands and to found colonies, consisting of himself, his father-in-law the ex-consul Appius, and his brother Gaius, then a very young man.

At this crisis Publius Scipio Nasica appeared. He was the grandson of the Scipio who had been adjudged by the Senate the best citizen of the state, the son of the Scipio who, as censor, had built the porticoes on the Capitol, and great-grandson of Gnaeus Scipio, that illustrious man who was the paternal uncle of Publius Scipio Africanus. Although he was a cousin of Tiberius Gracchus, he set his country before all ties of blood, choosing to regard as contrary to his private interests everything that was not for the public weal, a quality which earned for him the distinction of being the first man to be elected pontifex maximus *in absentia*. He held no public office at this time and was clad in the toga. Wrapping the fold of his toga about his left forearm, he stationed himself on the topmost steps of the Capitol and summoned all those who wished for the safety of the state to follow him. Then the optimates, the Senate, the larger and better part of the equestrian order, and those of the plebs who were not yet infected by pernicious theories rushed upon Gracchus as he stood with his bands in the area of the Capitol and was haranguing a throng assembled from almost every part of Italy. As Gracchus fled, and was running down the steps which led from the Capitol, he was struck by the fragment of a bench, and ended by an untimely death the life which he might have made a glorious one. This was the beginning in Rome of civil bloodshed, and of the licence of the sword. From this time on right was crushed by might, the most powerful now took precedence in the state, the disputes of the citizens which were once healed by amicable agreements were now settled by arms, and wars were now begun not for good cause but for what profit there was in them. Nor is this to be wondered at; for precedents do not stop where they begin, but, however narrow the path upon which they enter, they create for themselves a highway whereon they may wander with the utmost latitude; and when once the path of right is abandoned, men are hurried into wrong in headlong haste, nor does anyone think a course is base for himself which has proven profitable to others.

—VELLEIUS PATERCULUS, *Historia Romana* II.2–3, translated by Frederick W. Shipley

33 **ostendās**: subjunctive (without **ut**) with **oportēbit**. *__lūmen, lūminis__ (*n*), light.
ingenium, -ī (*n*), one's natural capacity, abilities, genius.
34 **eius temporis**: "of this time (of your life)," i.e., from the time of Scipio's return from
Numantia (133 B.C.) to his death in 129 B.C.
anceps, ancipitis, two-headed (**caput, capitis**), divided, branching in two directions,
uncertain. **videō**: the elder Scipio speaks as a prophet.
*__quasi__, as if, as it were. "I see a path branching in two directions as if (it were) the
path of the fates of this time (that await you at this time of your life)." I.e., this
is a period during which the younger Scipio will have to make difficult and fateful choices. There is an implied comparison here with Hercules at the crossroads
and with Achilles' choice between a short life with eternal fame or a long life
that would be forgotten (consult a mythological dictionary).
35 **septēnī, -ae, -a**, seven each, seven. **octiēns**, eight times. **septēnōs octiēns**: = 56,
Scipio's age as he narrates his dream in 129 B.C.
ānfractus, -ūs (*m*), a breaking round (**frangō, frangere**), bending, circuit, revolution.
*__reditus, -ūs__ (*m*), return, returning (**redeō, redīre**). **ānfractūs reditūsque**: "returning
circuits."
*__convertō, convertere__ (3), **convertī, conversum**, to turn back, turn.
36 **iī**: = **eī**. **plēnus**: "full," in the sense of "lacking nothing," "perfect." Seven and
eight were among the numbers regarded as sacred or perfect by the ancients. See
The Oxford Classical Dictionary, "Numbers, Sacred," p. 742.
alter alterā dē causā: ellipsis or compressed expression, common with **alter . . . alter**,
"the one for one reason, the other for another reason." The full wording would be
alter (plēnus habētur) dē alterā causā, alter dē alterā causā.
37 **circuitus, -ūs** (*m*), a going round, circuit, revolution. **summam . . . fātālem**: supply
annōrum.
in tē ūnum: Rome will look to the younger Scipio for guidance in this new crisis
just as it looked to his grandfather in the Second Punic War and as it would look
to Cicero himself during the Catilinarian conspiracy of 63 B.C.
38 **tē . . . tē . . . tē . . . tē** (39): note the *anaphora* (repetition of a word at the beginning
of successive phrases or clauses), emphasizing the breadth of support for and reli-
ance on Scipio in the political crisis following the murder of Tiberius Gracchus.
bonī: i.e., the conservative senatorial faction, the **Optimātēs**.
sociī . . . Latīnī (39): **Latīnī** was the name given to the peoples of the plain of La-
tium in their alliance with Rome, and the **sociī** were the other peoples of Italy, all
brought under Roman control (see *The Oxford Classical Dictionary*, "Latini," p.
582, and "Socii," p. 997).
39 *__intueor, intuērī__ (2), **intuitus sum**, to look at or toward, look to for help.
nītor, nītī (3), **nīsus** or **nixus sum**, to rest, rely, depend on. **nītātur**: subjunctive in a
relative clause of characteristic.
nē multa (40) (**dīcam**): "lest (I say) more," "in short."
40 **dictātor**: see *The Oxford Classical Dictionary*, "Dictator," p. 339.
dictātor . . . cōnstituās (*subjunctive dependent on* **oportet**): "it is necessary that you
as dictator restore, set in order. . . ."
impius, -a, -um, irreverent, unrespectful, wicked, impious.
41 **effugiō, effugere** (3), **effūgī**, to flee away, escape. **sī** (39) **. . . effūgeris**: this ominous
warning looks toward Scipio's death in 129 B.C. caused, according to rumor, by
foul play of relatives (one suspect being his wife Sempronia, sister of the Gracchi,
whose agrarian reforms he opposed). **exclāmō** (1), to cry out. Why is the subjunctive used here?
Laelius: C. Laelius Sapiens, a Roman statesman and philosopher and a longtime
friend of the younger Scipio. Laelius was one of the group of men to whom Scipio
is recounting his dream, and he here registers his shock and sorrow over the pre-
diction of his friend's death. For details of Laelius' career, see *The Oxford Classical Dictionary*, "Laelius," p. 576, and "Scipionic Circle," pp. 963–964.
ingemō, ingemere (3), **ingemuī**, to groan or sigh over a thing.
42 **lēniter**, gently. **arrīdeō, arrīdēre** (3), **arrīsī, arrīsum**, to laugh or smile at or upon.
st (*interjection*), hush!
*__quaesō, quaesere__ (3), to pray, beseech. Often used to soften a command: "please."
43 **excitō** (1), to call out or forth, rouse or wake up. **nē . . . excitētis**: jussive clause
introduced by **quaesō**. **parumper**, for a little while, for a moment.

A political crisis in Rome will challenge Scipio's genius and statesmanship.

33 **XII.** "Hīc tū, Āfricāne, ostendās oportēbit patriae lūmen animī ingeniīque
34 tuī cōnsiliīque. Sed eius temporis ancipitem videō quasi fātōrum viam.
35 Nam cum aetās tua septēnōs octiēns sōlis ānfractūs reditūsque converterit,
36 duoque iī numerī, quōrum uterque plēnus alter alterā dē causā habētur,
37 circuitū nātūrālī summam tibi fātālem cōnfēcerint, in tē ūnum atque in
38 tuum nōmen sē tōta convertet cīvitās; tē senātus, tē omnēs bonī, tē sociī,
39 tē Latīnī intuēbuntur; tū eris ūnus in quō nītātur cīvitātis salūs; ac, nē
40 multa, dictātor rem pūblicam cōnstituās oportet, sī impiās propinquōrum
41 manūs effūgeris." Hīc cum exclāmāvisset Laelius ingemuissentque
42 vehementius cēterī, lēniter arrīdēns Scīpiō, "St! Quaesō," inquit, "nē mē ē
43 somnō excitētis, et parumper audīte cētera."

1. **What will the political crisis in Rome demand of the younger Scipio?** (33–34)
2. **What kind of road does the elder Scipio see ahead for his adoptive grandson?** (34)
3. **In what terms does the elder Scipio indicate how old his adoptive grandson will be at this critical moment in his life?** (35–37)
4. **Why does the elder Scipio indicate the younger Scipio's age in such a roundabout manner?** (35–37)
5. **How will the people of Rome and Italy regard the younger Scipio?** (37–39)
6. **With what new office should he be entrusted, and what should he do?** (40)
7. **What may prevent him from carrying out his duties?** (40–41)
8. **Why does Laelius exclaim, and why do the others groan?** (41–42)
9. **Explain the humor in Scipio's reply.** (42–43)

SCIPIO'S LAST YEARS AND HIS DEATH

After all the defeats experienced [by the Romans] at Numantia, Publius Scipio Africanus Aemilianus, the destroyer of Carthage, was a second time elected consul and then dispatched to Spain, where he confirmed the reputation for good fortune and valor which he had earned in Africa. Within a year and three months after his arrival in Spain he surrounded Numantia with his siege works, destroyed the city and leveled it to the ground. No man of any nationality before his day had immortalized his name by a more illustrious feat of destroying cities; for by the destruction of Carthage and Numantia he liberated us, in the one case from fear, in the other from a reproach upon our name. This same Scipio, when asked by Carbo the tribune what he thought about the killing of Tiberius Gracchus, replied that he had been justly slain if his purpose had been to seize the government. When the whole assembly cried out at this utterance he said, "How can I, who have so many times heard the battle shout of the enemy without feeling fear, be disturbed by the shouts of men like you, to whom Italy is only a stepmother?" A short time after Scipio's return to Rome, in the consulship of Manius Aquilius and Gaius Sempronius . . . this man who had held two consulships, had celebrated two triumphs, and had twice destroyed cities which had brought terror to his

ROMAN GOVERNMENT (Late Republic)

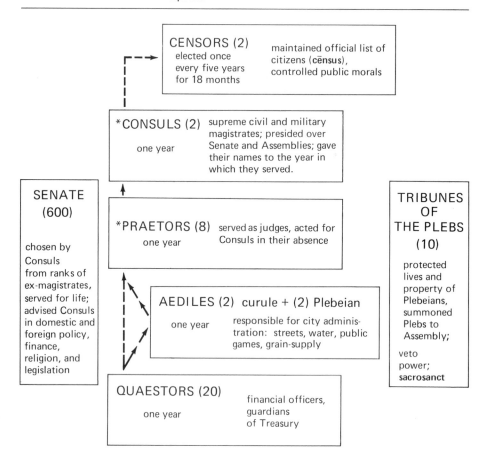

*DICTATOR

six months

possessed full powers, nominated by one of the Consuls when the Senate proclaimed a national emergency; chose his subordinate, the **magister equitum**

CENSORS (2)
elected once every five years for 18 months

maintained official list of citizens (cēnsus), controlled public morals

*CONSULS (2)

one year

supreme civil and military magistrates; presided over Senate and Assemblies; gave their names to the year in which they served.

SENATE (600)

chosen by Consuls from ranks of ex-magistrates, served for life; advised Consuls in domestic and foreign policy, finance, religion, and legislation

*PRAETORS (8)

one year

served as judges, acted for Consuls in their absence

AEDILES (2) curule + (2) Plebeian

one year

responsible for city administration: streets, water, public games, grain-supply

QUAESTORS (20)

one year

financial officers, guardians of Treasury

TRIBUNES OF THE PLEBS (10)

protected lives and property of Plebeians, summoned Plebs to Assembly;

veto power; **sacrosanct**

ASSEMBLIES OF THE PEOPLE

1. Comitia cūriāta

mostly Patricians, functions chiefly religious

2. Comitia centuriāta

elected higher magistrates, enacted laws, declared war

3. Comitia tribūta

Council of Plebeians, elected Tribunes and Plebeian Aediles

*Only these offices possessed **imperium**, supreme administrative power.

Cursus honōrum consisted of ranks of Quaestor, Praetor, and Consul.

Consuls and Praetors often subsequently became provincial administrators with the title Proconsul or Propraetor.

country, was found in the morning dead in his bed with marks as though of strangulation upon his throat. Great though he was, no inquest was held concerning the manner of his death, and with covered head was borne to the grave the body of him whose services had enabled Rome to lift her head above the whole world. Whether his death was due to natural causes as most people think, or was the result of a plot, as some historians state, the life he lived was at any rate so crowded with honors that up to this time it was surpassed in brilliance by none, excepting only his grandsire. He died in his fifty-sixth year.

—VELLEIUS PATERCULUS, *Historia Romana*, II.4, translated by Frederick W. Shipley

It is hard to speak of the nature of his death; you know what people suspect; yet I may say with truth that, of the many very joyous days which he saw in the course of his life—days thronged to the utmost with admiring crowds—the most brilliant was the day before he departed this life, when, after the adjournment of the Senate, he was escorted home toward evening by the Conscript Fathers, the Roman populace, and the Latin allies, so that from so lofty a station of human grandeur he seems to have passed to the gods on high rather than to the shades below.

—CICERO, *De amicitia* III.12, adapted from the translation of W. A. Falconer

A MODERN HISTORIAN'S RECONSTRUCTION OF SCIPIO'S LAST DAYS

By the end of 130 [B.C.] the complaints of the Italian allies about the activities of the agrarian commission had reached considerable proportions. . . . The complaints were seized upon by Scipio as a powerful weapon for use against the Gracchans. . . . In the early months of 129 Scipio began his attack, which evidently was planned to minimize the opposition step by step, instead of attacking the whole agrarian program at once. Scipio first laid a proposal before the Senate. Presumably this was the occasion of his speech against the *lex iudiciaria* of Tiberius Gracchus. . . . The Senate accepted the proposal. . . . This alone would have been sufficient to arouse the wrath of the Gracchans; but Scipio prepared to take the attack a stage further, probably by attempting actually to amend or repeal Tiberius' *lex iudiciaria*, and thereby formally to curtail or annul the judicial powers of the commissioners. The Gracchans, seeing in this a deliberate attempt to halt the redistribution of land, resisted vigorously. Tension rose. . . . At a *contio* Scipio faced a Gracchan mob shouting "kill the tyrant"—thus adopting the polemic of their opponents. His reply reveals much, both about himself and about the bitterness of the dispute: "Naturally those who are enemies of their own country wish to destroy me first; for Rome cannot fall while Scipio stands, nor Scipio live when Rome has fallen." It was on that same evening, it seems, that he was escorted home by a massive crowd of supporters. He retired to his room, intending, it is said, to compose another important speech, which was to be delivered the next day. In the morning he was found dead.

—A. E. ASTIN, *Scipio Aemilianus*, pp. 238–241

44 **quō**: = **ut** (in a purpose clause that contains a comparative adjective or adverb).
   tūtor, tūtārī (1), **tūtātus sum**, to protect, defend. **ad tūtandam rem pūblicam**: "to protect the state."
45 ***habētō** (*future imperative of* **habeō**): "consider," "be assured of this (sic)."
   cōnservō (1), to retain, maintain, preserve. Why are this and the following verbs in the subjunctive? What is the tense of the subjunctives, and why is this tense used here?
   adiuvō (1), to help, assist, support.
46 **dēfīniō** (4), to set bounds to, limit, define, designate. **esse . . . dēfīnītum**: infinitive in indirect statement after **sīc habētō** (44–45).
   beātus, -a, -um, happy, prosperous, blessed, fortunate (here in the sense of being untouched by any physical or spiritual pain).
   aevum, -ī (*n*), lifetime, age, eternity.
   *sempiternus, -a, -um, everlasting.
   fruor, fruī (3), **frūctus sum** (+ *abl.*), to enjoy. **fruantur**: subjunctive in a subordinate clause within an indirect statement.
47 **illī prīncipī deō**: this is the metaphysical, transcendent First Being of the Stoics (see *The Oxford Classical Dictionary*, "Stoa," pp. 1015–1016) and the ruling, life-sustaining principle of the universe.
   *mundus, -ī (*m*), earth, world, universe. **quod**: the antecedent is **nihil** (46).
48 **fīat**: subjunctive in a relative clause of characteristic.
   acceptus, -a, -um, welcome, agreeable, acceptable.
   *coetus, -ūs (*m*), a coming or meeting together, assembling, uniting. **concilia coetūs-que**: note the *alliteration*.
   sociō (1), to join or unite together, associate.
49 **rēctor, rēctōris** (*m*), leader, ruler.
   cōnservātor, cōnservātōris (*m*), keeper, preserver, defender.
   hinc, from here. **hinc profectī hūc revertuntur** (50): the Stoics taught that the soul had its origin in the fire of the divine ether or upper atmosphere and returned to this World Soul after death. This place of origin was commonly thought of as the highest and lightest part of the atmosphere where the fixed stars fed on eternal flame. The elder Scipio seems at this point in his discourse to be modifying this notion by implying that only statesmen set out from and return to that place.

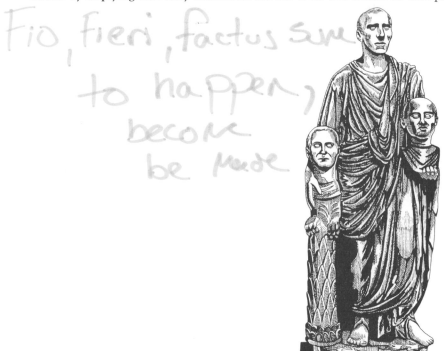

Marble statue of a Roman senator holding images of his ancestors.

18

The younger Scipio resumes his account of his dream. The elder Scipio continues his address to his adoptive grandson and encourages him with assurances that true statesmen find a place in heaven after their deaths.

44 **XIII.** "Sed quō sīs, Āfricāne, alacrior ad tūtandam rem pūblicam, sīc
45 habētō: omnibus quī patriam cōnservāverint, adiūverint, auxerint, certum
46 esse in caelō dēfīnītum locum, ubi beātī aevō sempiternō fruantur; nihil
47 est enim illī prīncipī deō, quī omnem mundum regit, quod quidem in
48 terrīs fīat, acceptius quam concilia coetūsque hominum iūre sociātī, quae
49 cīvitātēs appellantur; hārum rēctōrēs et cōnservātōrēs hinc profectī hūc
50 revertuntur."

1. **What is the elder Scipio attempting to do as he continues his discourse?** (44)
2. **By what three actions are true statesmen defined?** (45)
3. **What do true statesmen enjoy in heaven?** (46)
4. **How is the supreme god described?** (47)
5. **What activity of mankind is most pleasing to the supreme ruler of the universe?** (48)
6. **What kinds of people set out from and return to heaven?** (49–50)

THE MILKY WAY AS THE ULTIMATE ABODE OF THOSE *QUĪ PATRIAM CŌNSERVĀVĒRUNT, ADIŪVĒRUNT, AUXĒRUNT*

The souls of heroes, outstanding men deemed worthy of heaven, freed from the body and released from the globe of Earth, pass hither and, dwelling in a heaven that is their own, live the infinite years of paradise and enjoy celestial bliss. [There follows a long list of Greek and Roman heroes, statesmen, philosophers, generals, and rulers (including the Scipios) who have ascended to the Milky Way.] There [just above the Milky Way] is the gods' abode, and here [in the Milky Way] is theirs, who, peers of the gods in excellence, attain to the nearest heights.

—MANILIUS, *Astronomica* I.758–804, adapted from the translation of G. P. Goold

THE *CĪVITĀS* OR *RĒS PŪBLICA*: OBJECT OF THE STATESMAN'S CARE ON EARTH

A commonwealth is the property of a people. But a people is not any collection of human beings brought together in any sort of way, but an assemblage of people in large numbers associated in an agreement with respect to justice and a partnership for the common good. The first cause of such an association is not so much the weakness of the individual as a certain social spirit which nature has implanted in man. For man is not a solitary or unsocial creature, but born with such a nature that not even under conditions of great prosperity of every sort is he willing to be isolated from his fellow men.

—CICERO, *De republica* I.XXV.39, adapted from the translation of C. W. Keyes

Above: *Cn. Pompeius Magnus 106* B.C.–*58* B.C. Below: *C. Julius Caesar 100* B.C.–*44* B.C.

TRUE *RĒCTŌRĒS ET CŌNSERVĀTŌRĒS* OF THE COMMONWEALTH; A CONTRAST WITH THE AMBITIOUS GENERALS OF CICERO'S DAY

CICERO TO ATTICUS, GREETING (27 February 49 B.C.)

... So I spend my time considering the character of the ideal states-man, who is sketched clearly enough, you seem to think, in my books on the Republic. You remember then the standard by which our ideal governor (**moderātor reī pūblicae**) was to weigh his acts. Here are Scipio's words, in the fifth book. I think it is: "As a safe voyage is the aim of the pilot, health of the physician, victory of the general, so the ideal statesman will aim at happiness for the citizens of the state to give them material security, copious wealth, wide-reaching distinction and untarnished honor. This, the greatest and finest of human achievements, I want him to perform." Pompey never had this notion and least of all in the present cause. Absolute power is what he and Caesar have sought; their aim has not been to secure the happiness and honor of the community. Pompey has not abandoned Rome, because it was impossible to defend, nor Italy on forced compulsion; but it was his idea from the first to plunge the world into war, to stir up barbarous princes, to bring savage tribes into Italy under arms, and to gather a huge army. A sort of Sulla's reign has long been his object, and is the desire of many of his companions. Or do you think that no agreement, no compromise between him and Caesar was possible? Why, it is possible today: but neither of them looks to our happiness. Both want to be kings. . . .

—CICERO, *Letters to Atticus* VIII.XI, translated by E. O. Winstedt

L. Cornelius Sulla
138 B.C.–78 B.C.

52 **ā meīs**: "by my own (kinsmen)."
   ipse: i.e., Africanus Major.
   Paulus pater: Lucius Aemilius Paulus Macedonicus, father of the younger Scipio and
      conqueror of Greece, who ended the Third Macedonian War with his victory over
      Perseus at Pydna in 168 B.C. See *The Oxford Classical Dictionary*, "Paullus (2)
      Macedonicus," pp. 791-792.
53 *extinguō, extinguere (3), extinxī, extinctum**, to put out, extinguish, kill, destroy,
      annihilate.
   arbitrārēmur: subjunctive by attraction to the subjunctive of the indirect question
      (**vīveret**).
   immō, nay, rather. Here rejecting the assumption implied in **extinctōs . . . arbitrārē-
      mur**.
   *vērō**, in truth, certainly, surely.
54 **vinclum, -ī** (*n*), bond, rope, chains, fetters.
   tamquam, as if.
   carcer, carceris (*m*), prison.   **ē carcere . . . vīta** (55) **mors est**: according to the Pla-
      tonic conception, death, for lovers of wisdom, is a welcome liberation from the
      prison of the body and the beginning of true life (see Plato, *Phaedo* 67d).
   ēvolō (1), to fly out or away.
55 **Quīn**: introducing a question that suggests a command. The word heightens the
      dramatic color of the passage: "Why don't you look at . . . ?"
   *aspiciō, aspicere (3), aspexī, aspectum**, to look at, see.
56 **equidem**: emphasizes the 1st person singular subject ("I for my part. . . .").
   vim: "a flood."
   profundō, profundere (3), profūdī, profūsum, to pour forth.
57 **ōsculor, ōsculārī** (1), **ōsculātus sum**, to kiss. Is the present participle of a deponent
      verb active or passive in meaning?

As proof that true statesmen live and enjoy true life in heaven after their deaths, the younger Scipio's father, dead for over a decade, approaches and embraces his son.

51 **XIV.** Hīc ego, etsī eram perterritus nōn tam mortis metū quam
52 īnsidiārum ā meīs, quaesīvī tamen vīveretne ipse et Paulus pater et aliī
53 quōs nōs extinctōs esse arbitrārēmur. "Immō vērō," inquit, "hī vīvunt quī
54 ē corporum vinclīs tamquam ē carcere ēvolāvērunt, vestra vērō quae
55 dīcitur vīta mors est. Quīn tū aspicis ad tē venientem Paulum patrem?"
56 Quem ut vīdī, equidem vim lacrimārum profūdī, ille autem mē complexus
57 atque ōsculāns flēre prohibēbat.

1. **What is the younger Scipio's chief fear?** (51–52)
2. **What does he ask his adoptive grandfather?** (52–53)
3. **How does the elder Scipio describe what people normally call death?** (53–54)
4. **How can our life be called death?** (54–55) **How can what we call death be called life?** (53–55)
5. **The younger Scipio asks whether his father is still alive.** (52) **How is his question finally answered?** (55)
6. **How does the younger Scipio react when he sees his father?** (56) **How does his father respond?** (56–57)

VĪTA MORS EST

"Who knows if life be not death and death life?"

—EURIPIDES, quoted by Plato, *Gorgias* 492

"An vita mortalium mors potius quam vita dicenda sit"
"Whether the Life of Mortals Should Be Called Death Rather Than Life"

—ST. AUGUSTINE, *Civitas Dei*, title of Book XIII, Chapter 10

For some say that the body is the grave (σῆμα) of the soul which may be thought to be buried in our present life. Probably the Orphic poets were the inventors of the name, and they were under the impression that the soul is suffering the punishment of sin, and that the body is an enclosure or prison in which the soul is incarcerated, kept safe (σῶμα, σῴζηται), as the name σῶμα (body) implies, until the penalty is paid.

—PLATO, *Cratylus* 400, translated by B. Jowett

Socrates, on the very day on which he was to die, argues at length that this which we fancied to be life is really death, the soul being confined in the body as in a prison, while that was true life when this same soul, released from the bonds of the body, betook itself again to the place whence it sprang.

—CICERO, *Pro Scauro* III.4, translated by N. H. Watts

58 **ut prīmum**: "as soon as."
   flētus, -ūs (*m*), weeping.
   reprimō, reprimere (3), **repressī, repressum**, to press back, check, curb, restrain.
59 **sanctus, -a, -um**, sacred, pious, venerable.
   haec: i.e., "this state in which you exist."
60 **quid**: "why?"
   quīn, why . . . not?
61 **properō** (1), to hasten.
62 ***templum, -ī** (*n*), an open space in the sky marked out by the augur with his staff
   for a religious observance as he watches for omens, any open space, the entire
   sky, a sacred place, temple. Here Cicero plays on the double sense of "heavenly
   space" and "temple."
   ***custōdia, -ae** (*f*), guard, protection, custody, confinement, prison.   **istīs . . . custō-**
   diīs: ablative of separation, "from that confinement."
63 **hūc**: i.e., into the heavens.
   hāc lēge: "on this condition," "with this purpose."
   generō (1), to beget, produce, create.
64 **quī tuērentur**: relative clause of purpose.
   ***globus, -ī** (*m*), round body, sphere, globe.
   in hōc templō: the word **templum** here refers to the whole universe.
   medium: according to Cicero's cosmology, the earth is situated in the middle of the
   universe. This view prevailed in antiquity.
65 ***iīsque**: = **eīsque**.
   animus datus est: for the idea that souls of individuals derive from the eternal fires
   of the stars, see above, note on line 49 (**hinc profectī hūc revertuntur**).
   sīdus, sīderis (*n*), stars united in a figure, constellation.   **quae sīdera**: the relative
   pronoun **quae** is neuter plural by attraction to the gender of **sīdera**.
66 **animō** (1), to fill with breath or air, animate.   **dīvīnīs animātae mentibus**: just as
   our souls animate our bodies, so the World Soul animates the stars. Plato, Aristotle, and the Stoics thought that the stars were divine and possessed intelligence.
67 **circulus, -ī** (*m*), circle, circular course, orbit.
   ***orbis, orbis** (*m*), circle, orbit.
   ***mīrābilis, -is, -e**, wonderful, marvelous, extraordinary.
   quārē, for which reason, therefore.
68 **pius, -a, -um**, dutiful, conscientious, respectful, loyal.   **tibi** (67) . . . **piīs omnibus**:
   datives of agent with the gerundive **retinendus.**
   retineō, retinēre (2), **retinuī, retentum**, to hold back, keep.
   iniussū (*word used only in ablative*), without command.
69 **migrandum est**: impersonal construction, parallel to **retinendus est** and construed
   with **tibi . . . piīs omnibus** (67-68) as datives of agent.
70 **adsignō** (1), to assign, allot.
   dēfugiō, dēfugere (3), **dēfūgī**, to flee, shun, avoid.
   videāminī: what form of the verb is this? In what kind of a clause is it being used
   here?

The younger Scipio asks his father why, if the afterlife in heaven is the true life, men should not hasten there by committing suicide.

58 **XV.** Atque ego ut prīmum flētū repressō loquī posse coepī, "Quaesō,"
59 inquam, "pater sanctissime atque optime, quoniam haec est vīta, ut
60 Āfricānum audiō dīcere, quid moror in terrīs? Quīn hūc ad vōs venīre
61 properō?" "Nōn est ita," inquit ille. "Nisi enim cum deus is, cuius hoc
62 templum est omne quod cōnspicis, istīs tē corporis custōdiīs līberāverit,
63 hūc tibi aditus patēre nōn potest. Hominēs enim sunt hāc lēge generātī,
64 quī tuērentur illum globum quem in hōc templō medium vidēs, quae terra
65 dīcitur, iīsque animus datus est ex illīs sempiternīs ignibus quae sīdera et
66 stellās vocātis, quae globōsae et rotundae, dīvīnīs animātae mentibus,
67 circulōs suōs orbēsque cōnficiunt celeritāte mīrābilī. Quārē et tibi, Pūblī,
68 et piīs omnibus retinendus animus est in custōdiā corporis nec iniussū
69 eius ā quō ille est vōbīs datus, ex hominum vītā migrandum est, nē mūnus
70 hūmānum adsignātum ā deō dēfūgisse videāminī.

1. After hearing Africanus Major's words about the meaning of the term "life" (*vīta*, 52), what does the younger Scipio consider doing? (60–61)
2. How does his father react to his question? (61)
3. Upon what condition is access to the heavens open? (61–63)
4. For what purpose are men born? (64)
5. From where do the souls of men come? (65–67)
6. What animates the stars? (66)
7. At whose command may one depart from life? (68–69)
8. Why should men not depart from life of their own choice? (69–70)

THE DIVINE FIRE OF HEAVENLY BODIES AND OF THE HUMAN SOUL

We must assign divinity to the stars, which are formed from the most mobile and the purest part of the aether, and are not compounded of any other element besides; they are of a fiery heat and translucent throughout. Hence they have the fullest right to be pronounced to be living beings, endowed with sensation and intelligence. Now our ordinary fire that serves the needs of daily life is a destructive agency, consuming everything. On the other hand the fire of [the soul within] the body is the glow of life and health; it is the universal preservative, giving nourishment, fostering growth, sustaining, bestowing sensation. There can be no doubt which of the two kinds of fire the sun [and the other heavenly bodies] resemble, for the sun causes all things to flourish and to bring forth increase each after its kind. Hence the sun resembles those fires which are contained in the bodies of living creatures; and so too the other heavenly bodies, since they have their origin in the fiery heat of heaven that is entitled the aether or sky.

—CICERO, *De natura deorum* II.XV.39–41, adapted from the translation of H. Rackham

71 **avus, -ī** (*m*), grandfather.
   gignō, gignere (3), **genuī, genitum**, to beget.
   iūstitia, -ae (*f*), justice.
72 ***colō, colere** (2), **coluī, cultum**, to cultivate, tend, care for, practice, devote oneself
     to.
   pietās, pietātis (*f*), dutiful conduct, loyalty, patriotism.
   quae . . . magna in parentibus: "(this obligation) which is great in the case of par-
     ents."
   cum . . . tum, both . . . and.
   magna in parentibus et propinquīs . . . in patriā (73) **maxima**: an example of *chias-*
     mus, in which words or phrases are arranged in the pattern A B B A.
73 **Ea vīta via est in caelum**: the idea that the good life is a "road" to heaven was
     found among the Stoics and is seen as well in the Judaeo-Christian tradition.
     Plato and the Stoics asserted that the true home of the soul was the sky and that
     during life on earth the soul constantly aspires to return to its heavenly origin.
     The Stoics described this return as a homeward journey.
   vīta via . . . caelum . . . coetum: alliteration. **vīta via . . . vīxērunt** (74): note the
     play on words.
   quī iam (74) **vīxērunt**: note that Scipio does not say **quī mortuī sunt** because these
     people are regarded as still "alive," although they have completed (note the tense
     of the verb) one phase of their existence.
74 **laxō** (1), to open, undo, unloose (with ablative of separation).
75 **is**: with **circus.**
   splendidus, -a, -um, bright, shining, splendid. **splendidissimō candōre**: with **ēlūcēns.**
   candor, candōris (*m*), a dazzling whiteness, radiance, brightness, glitter.
   flammās: i.e., the stars.
   circus, -ī (*m*), circle. Here, of the Milky Way.
   ēlūceō, ēlūcēre (2), **ēlūxī**, to shine out, shine forth.
76 **Grāiī, -ōrum** (*m pl*) (*a less frequent and more poetic form for* **Graecī**), the Greeks.
     Grāīs: = **Grāiīs.**
   lacteus, -a, -um, of milk (**lac, lactis**), milky.
   nuncupō (1), to call, name.
   Ex quō: "From that point."
   omnia: i.e., the universe, object of **contemplantī** (77).
77 ***contemplō** (1), to survey, behold, observe, consider.
   praeclārus, -a, -um, very bright, clear.
   cētera: "the rest" (except the Milky Way from which Scipio is looking? or except
     the earth?—cf. lines 80–83).
78 **ex hōc locō**: i.e., from the earth.
79 **ea**: i.e., the moon; note that the word **stella** can be used of any of the celestial
     bodies.
80 **citimus, -a, -um** (*superlative of* **citer, citra, citrum**, near, close to), closest, very
     close.
   lūceō, lūcēre (2), **lūxī**, to shine. **lūce lūcēbat aliēnā**: the moon was known to shine
     with reflected light. Note the alliteration.
82 **punctum, -ī** (*n*), point, small spot. For **quasi**, "as if," introducing a comparison, cf.
   quasi fātōrum (34 and note). Be on the lookout for further comparisons introduced
     by **quasi.**
83 **paeniteō, paenitēre** (2), **paenituī**, to cause to repent, to displease. Usually used im-
     personally, e.g., **paenitet aliquem alicuius reī** = it repents one, it makes one re-
     gret, it makes one sorry about something (genitive). **mē imperiī nostrī . . .**
   paenitēret: "it made me sorry for our empire," "I felt sorry for, dissatisfied with,
     our empire." In what kind of a subordinate clause is the subjunctive being used
     here? What word in the main clause indicates that this kind of subordinate clause
     is coming?

Scipio's father explains that the life of virtue is the road to a heavenly dwelling place in the Milky Way.

71 **XVI.** "Sed sīc, Scīpiō, ut avus hic tuus, ut ego quī tē genuī, iūstitiam
72 cole et pietātem, quae cum magna in parentibus et propinquīs, tum in
73 patriā maxima est. Ea vīta via est in caelum et in hunc coetum eōrum quī
74 iam vīxērunt et corpore laxātī illum incolunt locum quem vidēs" (erat
75 autem is splendidissimō candōre inter flammās circus ēlūcēns), "quem vōs,
76 ut ā Grāis accēpistis, orbem lacteum nuncupātis." Ex quō omnia mihi
77 contemplantī praeclāra cētera et mīrābilia vidēbantur. Erant autem eae
78 stellae quās numquam ex hōc locō vīdimus, et eae magnitūdinēs omnium
79 quās esse numquam suspicātī sumus, ex quibus erat ea minima quae,
80 ultima ā caelō, citima ā terrīs, lūce lūcēbat aliēnā. Stellārum autem globī
81 terrae magnitūdinem facile vincēbant. Iam vērō ipsa terra ita mihi parva
82 vīsa est ut mē imperiī nostrī, quō quasi punctum eius attingimus,
83 paenitēret.

1. **What models does Paulus hold up to the younger Scipio for emulation?** (71)
2. **What virtues does he recommend, and what is their importance?** (71–73)
   To what do they lead? (73–74)
3. **From what have those who dwell in heaven been set free?** (74)
4. **How is the Milky Way described?** (74–75)
5. **From whom did the Romans get their name for the Milky Way?** (76)
6. **How did things appear to the younger Scipio as he gazed from his vantage point in the Milky Way?** (76–77)
7. **What did he see that he had never seen before?** (77–78)
8. **How large did the various bodies in the universe seem to be?** (78–79)
   Which seemed to be larger than one usually thinks? Which smaller? (77–80)
9. **What is the last thing that attracts the younger Scipio's attention as he surveys the universe?** (81–82) **What are his feelings about it?** (81–83)

IŪSTITIAM COLE ET PIETĀTEM

There is no social relation more close, none more dear than that which links each one of us with our country. Parents are dear; dear are children, relatives, friends; but one native land embraces all our loves; and who that is true would hesitate to give his life for her, if by his death he could render her a service? So much the more execrable are those monsters who have torn their fatherland to pieces with every form of outrage and who are* and have been** engaged in compassing her utter destruction.

—CICERO, *De officiis* I.XVIII.57, adapted from the translation of W. Miller

*Antony and his associates.   **Caesar, Clodius, Catiline.

84 **Quam**: i.e., the earth.

magis: "more intently."

intuērer: what tense of the subjunctive, and why is the subjunctive being used here?

quōusque, until when, how long.

85 **humī**, on the ground.

dēfīgō, dēfīgere (3), **dēfīxī, dēfīxum**, to fasten, fix upon.

Nōnne aspicis: at this point the elder Scipio explains to the younger Scipio the organization and workings of the universe according to the popular astronomy (and astrology) of the ancient world. The concept is that of eight concentric orbits or spheres with the earth as the ninth element in the scheme, fixed and immovable at the center. The theory was accepted for more than thirteen centuries.

quae in templa vēneris: what kind of a clause?

86 **tibi**: dative of reference, "you must know."

potius (*adv.*), rather.

cōnectō, cōnectere (3), **cōnexuī, cōnexum**, to tie, bind, fasten, join together.

87 **caelestis, -is, -e**, heavenly, celestial. **ūnus** (86) . . . **caelestis**: this is the outermost sphere of the fixed stars.

extimus, -a, -um, outermost.

88 **arceō, arcēre** (2), **arcuī, arctum**, to shut in, enclose.

īnfīgō, īnfīgere (3), **īnfīxī, īnfīxum**, to fix or fasten in.

volvō, volvere (3), **volvī, volūtum**, to roll, turn about, (here passive in reflexive sense) turn or roll oneself round about, turn or roll along.

89 **subiciō, subicere** (3), **subiēcī, subiectum**, to throw, lay, place, bring under.

septem: the next seven spheres are those of the planets Saturn, Jupiter, and Mars, the sun, the planets Venus and Mercury, and the moon.

versō (1), to turn, whirl about, (here passive in reflexive sense) turn oneself, turn, revolve.

retrō, backwards.

contrārius, -a, -um, opposite, contrary.

contrāriō . . . **atque** (90) **caelum**: "opposite to (the sphere of) the heavens"; **atque** (**ac**) is often used to mean "than," "as," or "to" after comparisons or adjectives and adverbs of likeness or difference.

90 **possideō, possidēre** (2), **possēdī, possessum**, to have and hold, possess.

illa (**stella**): "that (planet)."

91 **Saturnius, -a, -um**, of or belonging to Saturn. **Saturnia** (**stella**): "the planet Saturn."

prosperus, -a, -um, agreeable to one's wishes, favorable, fortunate.

salūtāris, -is, -e, healthful, wholesome, beneficial, advantageous. **prosperus et salūtāris**: according to ancient astrologers, the planets influenced human lives.

92 **fulgor, fulgōris** (*m*), gleam, brightness, splendor. Abstract for concrete: = **fulgēns stella.**

Iuppiter, Iovis (*m*), Jupiter, king of the gods.

rutilus, -a, -um, red.

horribilis, -is, -e, terrible, fearful, dreadful. Repeat **fulgor** as the noun modified by the adjectives **rutilus** and **horribilis.**

Martius, -a, -um, of or belonging to Mars (the god of war).

Scipio Africanus Major resumes his discourse by calling the younger Scipio's attention away from earthly concerns.

84 **XVII.** Quam cum magis intuērer, "Quaesō," inquit Āfricānus, "quōusque
85 humī dēfīxa tua mēns erit? Nōnne aspicis quae in templa vēneris? Novem
86 tibi orbibus vel potius globīs cōnexa sunt omnia, quōrum ūnus est
87 caelestis, extimus, quī reliquōs omnēs complectitur, summus ipse deus
88 arcēns et continēns cēterōs; in quō sunt īnfīxī illī quī volvuntur stellārum
89 cursūs sempiternī; cui subiectī sunt septem, quī versantur retrō contrāriō
90 mōtū atque caelum; ex quibus ūnum globum possidet illa quam in terrīs
91 Sāturniam nōminant. Deinde est hominum generī prosperus et salūtāris
92 ille fulgor quī dīcitur Iovis; tum rutilus horribilisque terrīs quem Martium
93 dīcitis;   *(passage continued on page 31)*

1. **For what does the elder Scipio reprimand his adoptive grandson?** (84–85)
2. **How are all things in the universe joined together?** (85–86)
3. **How is the outermost sphere of the universe described?** (86–89)
4. **In what direction do the spheres move that are below the outermost sphere (the *caelum*)?** (89–90)
5. **How many spheres are there in all?** (85–101)

THE AWESOME HEAVENS ABOVE US

When we gaze upward to the sky and contemplate the heavenly bodies, what can be so obvious and so manifest as that there must exist some power possessing transcendent intelligence by whom these things are ruled? Were it not so, how comes it that the words of Ennius carry conviction to all readers—

Behold this dazzling vault of heaven, which all mankind as Jove invoke,

ay, and not only as Jove but as sovereign of the world, ruling all things with his nod, and as Ennius likewise says—

father of gods and men.

—CICERO, *De natura deorum* II.II.4, translated by H. Rackham

94 **subter** (*adv.*), below, beneath.

95 **moderātor, moderātōris** (*m*), ruler, governor, director.

lūminum: here of the celestial bodies.

temperātiō, temperātiōnis (*f*), due mingling or tempering of ingredients, fit proportion, symmetry, temperament. Here used of the sun (note abstract for the concrete, **temperātor**) as the organizing or ordering principle in the universe in that it controls the regular alternation of days and nights and seasons of the year.

tantā magnitūdine (96): ablative of description. **tantā**: anticipating the result clause which follows.

96 *****cūnctus, -a, -um**, all. **lūstrō** (1), to purify, go around, wander over, survey, illuminate. **lūce lūstret**: note the alliteration.

*****compleō, complēre** (2), **complēvī, complētum**, to fill up.

comes, comitis (*m*), companion, (here) satellite.

97 **Venus, Veneris** (*f*), Venus. **Mercurius, -ī** (*m*), Mercury.

*****īnfimus, -a, -um**, lowest.

98 *****radius, -ī** (*m*), beam, ray.

accendō, accendere (3), **accendī, accēnsum**, to set on fire, light up, illuminate.

*****convertō, convertere** (3), **convertī, conversum**, to turn or whirl around, (here passive in reflexive sense) turn oneself around, revolve.

īnfrā, below. **Īnfrā autem**: the idea of the sublunar region being the region of earthly elements and the only region where qualitative changes such as birth and death can occur is found in Aristotle's *De caelo* III and IV.

*****mortālis, -is, -e**, subject to death (**mors, mortis**), mortal.

99 **cadūcus, -a, -um**, that falls, has fallen (from **cadō, cadere**), destined to die, frail, fleeting.

100 *****aeternus, -a, -um**, everlasting, eternal.

tellūs, tellūris (*f*), globe, the earth. Here *personified*, Tellus.

101 *****movētur**: here passive in reflexive sense, "does (not) move itself," "does (not) move."

nūtus, -ūs (*m*), nod, nodding, command, downward tendency or pull, gravity. **nūtū suō**: the force of gravity that draws all matter toward the center of the earth and, for the ancients, the center of the universe. To what does **suō** refer?

pondus, ponderis (*n*), heaviness, weight, mass.

Right: *The system of the world according to the ideas prevalent in the Middle Ages. Above the flat earth the sky forms a vault studded with stars. An inquisitive traveler puts his head through the vault and discovers the complicated mechanism that moves the stars.*

94   deinde subter mediam ferē regiōnem Sōl obtinet, dux et prīnceps et
95   moderātor lūminum reliquōrum, mēns mundī et temperātiō, tantā
96   magnitūdine ut cūncta suā lūce lūstret et compleat. Hunc ut comitēs
97   cōnsequuntur Veneris alter, alter Mercuriī cursus, in īnfimōque orbe Lūna
98   radiīs Sōlis accēnsa convertitur. Īnfrā autem iam nihil est nisi mortāle et
99   cadūcum praeter animōs mūnere deōrum hominum generī datōs, suprā
100 Lūnam sunt aeterna omnia. Nam ea quae est media et nōna, Tellūs, neque
101 movētur et īnfima est et in eam feruntur omnia nūtū suō pondera."

6.   **What interests the elder Scipio about each of the following? (a) Jupiter, (b) Mars, (c) the sun, (d) Venus and Mercury, (e) the moon** (91–98)

7.   **What is the only thing on earth that is not doomed to decay and death?** (99)

8.   **In what ways is the earth unique within the universe?** (98–101)

LŪNA RADIĪS SŌLIS ACCĒNSA

The moon, which is, as the mathematicians prove, more than half the size of the earth, roams in the same courses as the sun, but at one time converging with the sun and at another diverging from it, both bestows upon the earth the light that it has borrowed from the sun and itself undergoes divers changes of its light, and also at one time is in conjunction and hides the sun, darkening the light of its rays, at another itself comes into the shadow of the earth, being opposite to the sun, and owing to the interposition and interference of the earth is suddenly extinguished.

—CICERO, *De natura deorum* II.XL.103, translated by H. Rackham

102 **Quae**: to what in the previous passage does this linking pronoun refer?
   stupeō, stupēre (2), **stupuī**, to be struck senseless, be astonished, amazed.
   ut mē recēpī: "when I regained my senses." **recipiō, recipere** (3), **recēpī, receptum**,
      to regain, recover.
103 *****auris, auris** (*f*), ear. **dulcis, -is, -e**, sweet. *****sonus, -ūs** (*m*), noise, sound.
   Hic est . . . ille (104) (**sonus**): i.e., the music of the spheres.
104 *****intervallum, -ī** (*n*), space between, interval, distance.
   disiunctus, -a, -um, separate, apart, distinct. Construction: **disiunctus inter-**
      vallīs imparibus, sed tamen ratiōne (105) **distinctīs**. **intervallīs**: modified by **im-**
      paribus and **distinctīs**.
   impār, imparis, uneven, unequal, dissimilar.
   ratus, -a, -um, fixed, established, firm. **prō ratā parte**: "according to a fixed part,"
      "in proportion," "proportionally."
105 **ratiōne**: "according to reason," "rationally." *****distinctus, -a, -um**, separate, distinct.
   impulsus, -ūs (*m*), a pushing or striking against, pressure, impulse.
   *****acūtus, -a, -um**, sharp, pointed, (of sounds) high-pitched.
106 **gravis, -is, -e**, heavy, (of sounds) low-pitched. **acūta cum** (105) **gravibus**: "high-
      pitched with low-pitched notes."
   temperō (1), to mingle in due proportion, temper. **varius, -a, -um**, diverse, variegated.
   aequābiliter, uniformly, equally.
   concentus, -ūs (*m*) (*from* **con** + **canō, canere**, to sing), sounds blending harmoni-
      ously together, harmony, harmonious music.
107 **fert**: "allows," "permits" (followed by a substantive **ut** clause expressing result).
   extrēma: "the extremes."
108 **graviter**, (of music) low-pitched. **acūtē**, (of music) high-pitched.
   sonō, sonāre (1), **sonuī, sonitum**, to make a noise, sound, resound.
   summus . . . īnfimus (110): locate the elements of a chiasmus framed by these
      words.
109 **stellifer, stellifera, stelliferum**, star-bearing, starry.
   *****conversiō, conversiōnis** (*f*), a turning around, revolving, revolution.
   concitātus, -a, -um, quick, rapid.
   excitātus, -a, -um, aroused, animated, lively, strong, loud.
110 **lūnāris, -is, -e**, of or belonging to the moon.
111 **immōbilis, -is, -e**, unmoved, unmoving.
   *****sēdēs, sēdis** (*f*), seat, dwelling place, location.
   haereō, haerēre (2), **haesī, haesum**, to hold fast, be fixed, sit fast in a place (+ abla-
      tive). Note that since the earth does not move it makes no sound.
112 **septem . . . quī** (113) **numerus . . . nōdus** (114) **est**: the whirling spheres sound the
      seven notes of the musical scale; for the importance of the number seven, see
      note on line 36 (**plēnus**).
114 **nōdus, -ī** (*m*), knot.
   quod: i.e., this harmony of the spheres and the way in which it is produced.
   doctus, -a, -um, learned, skilled, experienced. **doctī hominēs**: "musicians."
   nervus, -ī (*m*), sinew, nerve, string of a musical instrument. On the strings of the
      seven-stringed lyre, musicians imitate nature's own perfect music.
   imitor, imitārī (1), **imitātus sum**, to imitate, copy.
   cantus, -ūs (*m*), song, singing, playing, music.
115 **praestāns, praestantis**, preeminent, superior, extraordinary.
   ingenium, -ī (*n*), one's natural capacity, abilities, genius.
   vītā hūmānā (116) **dīvīna studia**: chiasmus.
116 **dīvīna studia coluērunt**: "have pursued studies about heavenly things." Philosophers
      and astronomers, having attuned their minds to heavenly things, have prepared
      their souls for a return to their heavenly origins just as surely as have the musi-
      cians, who have made harmonious and heavenly music with their seven-stringed
      lyres.

The elder Scipio continues by explaining the music of the spheres.

102 **XVIII.** Quae cum intuērer stupēns, ut mē recēpī, "Quid? Hic," inquam,
103 "quis est, quī complet aurēs meās tantus et tam dulcis sonus?" "Hic est,"
104 inquit, "ille quī intervallīs disiunctus imparibus, sed tamen prō ratā parte
105 ratiōne distinctīs, impulsū et mōtū ipsōrum orbium efficitur et acūta cum
106 gravibus temperāns variōs aequābiliter concentūs efficit; nec enim silentiō
107 tantī mōtūs incitārī possunt et nātūra fert ut extrēma ex alterā parte
108 graviter, ex alterā autem acūtē sonent. Quam ob causam summus ille caelī
109 stellifer cursus, cuius conversiō est concitātior, acūtō et excitātō movētur
110 sonō, gravissimō autem hic lūnāris atque īnfimus. Nam terra, nōna,
111 immōbilis manēns ūnā sēde semper haeret complexa medium mundī
112 locum. Illī autem octō cursūs, in quibus eadem vīs est duōrum, septem
113 efficiunt distinctōs intervallīs sonōs, quī numerus rērum omnium ferē
114 nōdus est; quod doctī hominēs nervīs imitātī atque cantibus aperuērunt
115 sibi reditum in hunc locum, sīcut aliī quī praestantibus ingeniīs in vītā
116 hūmānā dīvīna studia coluērunt.

1. **How has the younger Scipio been affected by his survey of the spheres?** (102)
2. **What attracts his attention next?** (102–103)
3. **In what rational way is harmony produced by the sounds of the various
   spheres?** (103–106)
4. **Which sphere is the highest pitched?** (108–110) **Which the lowest?** (110)
5. **Which body in the universe makes no sound?** (110–112)
6. **Of how many tones altogether is the music of the spheres composed?** (112–113)
7. **How is this number described?** (113–114)
8. **Where in this passage does the elder Scipio suggest that art is an imitation of
   nature?**

PYTHAGORAS, THE MUSIC OF THE SPHERES, AND THE IDEAL STATESMAN

Music is united with the knowledge of things divine. Some of those
men whose wisdom is a household word have been earnest students of
music. Pythagoras, for instance, and his followers popularized the belief, which they no doubt had received from earlier teachers, that the
universe is constructed on the same principles which were afterwards
imitated in the construction of the lyre, and not content merely with
emphasizing that concord of discordant elements which they style harmony, he attributed a sound to the motions of the celestial bodies. It
was not therefore without reason that Plato regarded the knowledge of
music as necessary to his ideal statesman or politician, as he calls
him; while the Stoics held that the wise man might well devote some
of his attention to such studies.

—QUINTILIAN, *Institutio oratoria* I.X.10–15, adapted from the translation of
H. E. Butler

117 *sonitus, -ūs (m), sound.
    oppleō, opplēre (2), **opplēvī, opplētum**, to fill up.
    obsurdēscō, obsurdēscere (3), **obsurduī**, to become deaf (to something).
    hebes, hebetis, blunt, dull, dim, faint, (here perhaps) more easily weakened, more
        easily deadened.
118 *sēnsus, -ūs (m), perception, sensation, sense.
    Catadūpa, -ōrum (n pl) (a Greek word meaning "falling with a loud heavy sound"),
        the celebrated cataract of the Nile (near Syene, on the southern border of Egypt).
119 **praecipitō** (1), to throw or cast down headlong, rush or fall down.
    accolō, accolere (3), **accoluī, accultum**, to dwell by or near.
120 **careō** (2) (+ abl.), to be without, lack.
121 **incitātus, -a, -um**, rapid, swift.   **incitātissimā conversiōne**: "because of the very
    rapid revolution."
122 **capere**: "to perceive."
    possint: subjunctive in what kind of a clause?
    adversum (adv.), opposite to, against, toward, directly at.
    nequeō, nequīre (irreg.), **nequīvī** or **nequiī**, not to be able, to be unable.
    eiusque: -que, but.
123 **aciēs, aciēī** (f), sharp edge, point, keeness of vision, sight.   **aciēs . . . sēnsusque**: "the
    sense (or power) of sight" (hendiadys, two nouns used to express one idea).
    admīror, admīrārī (1), **admīrātus sum**, to wonder at, be astonished at.
    *referō, referre (irreg.), **rettulī, relātum**, to bring back, return.
124 **identidem**, repeatedly.

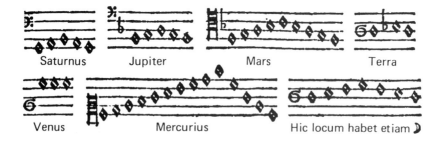

Musical notation based on Kepler's Harmonice Mundi, *showing the individual tunes played by the planets, the pitch of a note being proportional to the speed of the planet.*

The ancient philosopher and mathematician, Pythagoras, appears in this relief on Chartres cathedral in France. He took delight in perfect circles and relating musical scales to the planets.

34

Why do earthly mortals not hear the music of the spheres?

117 "Hōc sonitū opplētae aurēs hominum obsurduērunt; nec est ūllus hebetior
118 sēnsus in vōbīs, sīcut ubi Nīlus ad illa quae Catadūpa nōminantur
119 praecipitat ex altissimīs montibus, ea gēns quae illum locum accolit
120 propter magnitūdinem sonitūs sēnsū audiendī caret. Hic vērō tantus est
121 tōtīus mundī incitātissimā conversiōne sonitus ut eum aurēs hominum
122 capere nōn possint, sīcut intuērī sōlem adversum nequītis eiusque radiīs
123 aciēs vestra sēnsusque vincitur." Haec ego admīrāns referēbam tamen
124 oculōs ad terram identidem.

1. **What two different reasons does the elder Scipio give in this passage as to why men are normally not aware of the music of the spheres?** (117–120, 120–123)
2. **What is peculiar about the people of Catadupa?** (119–120)
3. **How convincingly does the inability to look directly at the sun illustrate the inability to hear the music of the spheres?** (120–123)
4. **How much interest does the younger Scipio take in the music of the spheres?** (123–124)

A DISSENTING OPINION ABOUT THE MUSIC OF THE SPHERES

The theory that music is produced by the movements [of the heavenly bodies], because the sounds they make are harmonious, although ingeniously and brilliantly formulated by its authors, does not contain the truth. It seems to some thinkers that bodies so great must inevitably produce a sound by their movement: even bodies on the earth do so, although they are neither so great in bulk nor moving at so high a speed, and as for the sun and the moon, and the stars, so many in number and enormous in size, all moving at a tremendous speed, it is incredible that they should fail to produce a noise of surpassing loudness. Taking this as their hypothesis, and also that the speeds of the stars, judged by their distances, are in the ratios of the musical consonances, they affirm that the sound of the stars as they revolve is concordant. To meet the difficulty that none of us is aware of this sound, they account for it by saying that the sound is with us right from birth and has thus no contrasting silence to show it up; for voice and silence are perceived by contrast with each other, and so all mankind is undergoing an experience like that of a copper-smith, who becomes by long habit indifferent to the din around him. Now this theory, I repeat, shows great feeling for fitness and beauty, but nevertheless it cannot be true. The difficulty of our hearing nothing, which they attempt to solve, is not the only one; there is also the absence of other effects unconnected with sensation. Excessively loud sounds are also able to shatter inanimate masses, e.g., the noise of thunder splits stones and other materials of the most enduring kinds. And when so many bodies are in motion, if the noise which travels here is in proportion to the size of the moving body, it must be many times greater than thunder when it reaches us, and of insupportable force and violence. No, there is a good reason why we neither hear anything ourselves nor see violence done to inanimate objects, namely that the movement is noiseless.

—ARISTOTLE, *On the Heavens* II.IX., adapted from the translation of W. K. C. Guthrie

125 **etiam nunc:** "even now" (after the unbelievable marvels I have shown you).
126 **contemplor, contemplārī** (1), **contemplātus sum,** to look at.
127 **caelestia, caelestium** (*n pl*), heavenly objects, divine things.
  spectātō: future imperative. **contemnitō:** future imperative.
128 **celebritās, celebritātis** (*f*), fame, renown, celebrity.
  expetō, expetere (3), **expetīvī** or **expetiī, expetītum,** to long for, seek after, aspire to.
  expetendam: "that is to be sought," "that is worth seeking."
129 **Vidēs . . . potestis** (133): which infinitives in this sentence are governed by **vidēs**? Which are not?
  habitārī in terrā: impersonal use of the passive infinitive: "(it) to be inhabited on the earth" = "that the earth is inhabited."
  rārus, -a, -um, having wide gaps between its parts, far apart, here and there, scattered.
130 **macula, -ae** (*f*), spot, mark, stain, blot.
  vastus, -a, -um, empty, unoccupied, immense, enormous, vast.
  solitūdō, solitūdinis (*f*), loneliness, solitariness, deserted place, wilderness.
  intericiō, intericere (3), **interiēcī, interiectum,** to throw, cast, or place between. With **interiectās** supply **esse**.
131 **nōn modo:** "not only," followed here by **sed** (132) **partim . . . partim . . . partim. . . .**
  interrumpō, interrumpere (3), **interrūpī, interruptum,** to break apart, scatter about.
132 **mānō** (1), to flow, spread. **possit:** subjunctive in what kind of a clause?
  partim (*adv.*), partly.
  oblīquus, -a, -um, sidelong, slanting, awry, oblique. **oblīquōs:** these would be the people who inhabit the other temperate zone of the same hemisphere.
  trānsversus, -a, -um, turned across, crosswise. **trānsversōs:** these would be the people who inhabit the same temperate zone of the other hemisphere.
133 *__adversus, -a, -um,__ turned to or toward a thing, standing over against, opposite.
  adversōs: these would be the people who inhabit the other temperate zone of the other hemisphere.

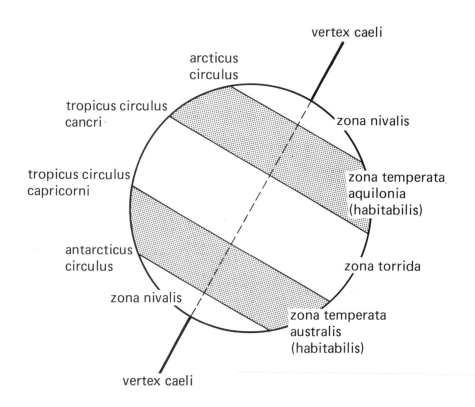

Zones of the earth as described by Scipio.

It is vain to try to achieve earthly glory or fame.

125 **XIX.** Tum Āfricānus, "Sentiō," inquit, "tē sēdem etiam nunc hominum
126 ac domum contemplārī; quae sī tibi parva, ut est, ita vidētur, haec
127 caelestia semper spectātō, illa hūmāna contemnitō. Tū enim quam
128 celebritātem sermōnis hominum aut quam expetendam cōnsequī glōriam
129 potes? Vidēs habitārī in terrā rārīs et angustīs in locīs, et in ipsīs quasi
130 maculīs ubi habitātur vastās solitūdinēs interiectās, eōsque quī incolunt
131 terram nōn modo interruptōs ita esse ut nihil inter ipsōs ab aliīs ad aliōs
132 mānāre possit, sed partim oblīquōs, partim trānsversōs, partim etiam
133 adversōs stāre vōbīs, ā quibus expectāre glōriam certē nūllam potestis.

1. **What does the elder Scipio notice that the younger Scipio is doing?** (125–126)
2. **According to the elder Scipio, does the earth merely seem small or is it really small?** (126)
3. **What actions does he urge the younger Scipio to take in response to this fact?** (126–127)
4. **On what grounds does he argue that glory is not worth seeking?** (127–133)
5. **What lies between the inhabited spots on the earth?** (130)
6. **What two reasons does the elder Scipio give to explain why communication cannot occur between different areas of the earth?** (130–133)
7. **Do you think that the immense changes made in modern times in transportation, communication, and the media would change the elder Scipio's attitude toward the importance of glory? To what extent is a person's fame still limited by geography or national boundaries?**

HAEC CAELESTIA SEMPER SPECTĀTŌ, ILLA HŪMĀNA CONTEMNITŌ

The mind of the philosopher, disdaining the littleness and nothingness of human things, is "flying all abroad" as Pindar says, measuring earth and heaven and the things which are under and on the earth and above the heaven, interrogating the whole nature of each and all in their entirety, but not condescending to anything which is within reach. Then how can he who has magnificence of mind and is the spectator of all time and all existence think much of human life?

—PLATO, *Theatetus* 173, and *Republic* VI.486, adapted from the translation of B. Jowett

The mind possesses the full and complete benefit of its human existence only when it spurns all evil, seeks the lofty and the deep, and enters the innermost secrets of nature. Then as the mind wanders among the very stars, it delights in laughing at the mosaic floors of the rich and at the whole earth with all its gold. I do not mean only the gold which the earth has already produced and surrendered to be struck for money but also all the gold the earth has preserved hidden away for the avarice of future generations. The mind cannot despise colonnades, panelled ceilings gleaming with ivory, trimmed shrubbery, and streams made to approach mansions, until it goes around the entire universe and looking down upon the earth from above (an earth limited and covered mostly by sea—while even the part out of the sea is squalid or parched and frozen) says to itself: "Is this that pinpoint which is divided by sword and fire among so many nations? How ridiculous are the boundaries of mortals!" That is a mere pinpoint on

134 **redimiō, redimīre** (4), **redimiī, redimītum**, to bind round, encircle, gird.
135 **cingulum, -ī** (*n*), girdle, belt, zone (of the earth). The conception of the earth being divided into five zones (three uninhabitable and two habitable) is attributed to Parmenides (mid-fifth century B.C.) and was elaborated by Aristotle and the Greek astronomer Eratosthenes (275–194 B.C.).
  dīversus, -a, -um, turned different ways, set over against each other, opposite. **duōs . . . dīversōs**: i.e., the north and south poles of the earth.
136 *****vertex, verticis** (*m*), whirlpool, coil of flame, highest point, summit, (plural) poles of the heavens, projections of the earth's axis.
  subnīxus, -a, -um, supported from beneath, propped up, resting on (+ ablative).
  obrigēscō, obrigēscere (3), **obriguī**, to stiffen, become hard.
  pruīna, -ae (*f*), frost.
137 **autem** (*adversative*), while on the other hand.
  maximus, -a, -um, broadest, widest.
  ardor, ardōris (*m*), flame, fire, heat.
  torreō, torrēre (2), **torruī, tostum**, to dry a thing by heat, parch, burn, scorch.
138 **austrālis, -is, -e**, southern (from **auster, austrī**, *m*, the south wind).
  īnsistō, īnsistere (3), **īnstitī**, to set foot upon, stand upon.
  urgeō, urgēre (2), **ursī**, to press.
  *****vēstigium, -ī** (*n*), footstep, step. **adversa vōbīs urgent vēstīgia**: "they plant their feet opposite to yours," i.e., they walk upside down in relation to you.
139 **nihil ad vestrum genus** (**pertinet**): "has no connection with your race (of men)."
  subiectus, -a, -um, lying under.
  *****aquilō, aquilōnis** (*m*), north wind, north. **subiectus aquilōnī**: a poetic phrase for the northern zone.
140 **quam**: with **tenuī . . . parte**, introducing an indirect question.
  tenuis, -is, -e, thin, slight, insignificant.
  contingō, contingere (3), **contigī, contactum**, to touch. **vōs . . . contingat**: "it touches you," "it is yours."
141 **angustō** (1), to make narrow.
  verticibus: "from top to bottom," i.e., from north to south.
  lateribus: "from side to side," i.e., from east to west. The northern temperate zone, which we inhabit, is compared to an island wider from east to west than from north to south and surrounded by Ocean.
  quaedam: introducing a metaphorical statement. **quaedam īnsula**: "a kind of island" or "like an island."
142 **circumfundō, circumfundere** (3), **circumfūsī, circumfūsum**, to pour around. **circumfūsus, -a, -um**, surrounded.
  Atlanticus, -a, -um, of or belonging to Mt. Atlas. The adjective refers to the ocean that extends out from the north African coast where Mt. Atlas is located.
  quem Ōceanum: the gender of the relative pronoun is attracted to that of **Ōceanum**.
  Ōceanus, -ī (*m*) (*Greek loan word*), a mythological figure, son of Uranus (Heaven) and Ge (Earth), husband of Tethys (goddess of the sea), and father of river gods and nymphs; (also) the sea or ocean that was thought to surround the known world.
143 **quī tamen tantō nōmine**: "which (although) of such a great name. . . ." Ablative of description.
  quam: introducing what kind of a clause?

which you navigate, on which you wage war, on which you arrange tiny kingdoms—tiny, even though ocean does run to meet them on both sides.

—SENECA, *Naturales quaestiones* I, Pref. 7–11, adapted from the translation of T. H. Corcoran

Africanus shows Scipio the different zones surrounding the globe and points out the insignificant segment inhabited by the Romans.

134 **XX.** "Cernis autem eandem terram quasi quibusdam redimītam et
135 circumdatam cingulīs, ē quibus duōs maximē inter sē dīversōs et caelī
136 verticibus ipsīs ex utrāque parte subnīxōs obriguisse pruīnā vidēs, medium
137 autem illum et maximum sōlis ardōre torrērī. Duo sunt habitābilēs,
138 quōrum austrālis ille, in quō quī īnsistunt adversa vōbīs urgent vēstīgia,
139 nihil ad vestrum genus; hic autem alter subiectus aquilōnī, quem incolitis,
140 cerne quam tenuī vōs parte contingat. Omnis enim terra quae colitur ā
141 vōbīs, angustāta verticibus, lateribus lātior, parva quaedam īnsula est,
142 circumfūsa illō marī quod Atlanticum, quod magnum, quem Ōceanum
143 appellātis in terrīs, quī tamen tantō nōmine quam sit parvus vidēs.

1. **Which are the two most widely separated zones of the earth?** (134–136)
2. **How are they described?** (134–136)
3. **What is the largest zone, and how is it described?** (136–137)
4. **Of what importance to the Romans is the southern habitable zone?** (138–139)
5. **How large or important does the part of the world inhabited by the Romans appear?** (139–140) **To what is it compared?** (141)
6. **What is actually small despite its great name?** (142–143)
7. **How does Cicero use metaphors and colorful, graphic details to clarify his description of the world and to make it more vivid?**

THE GEOGRAPHY OF THE WORLD AS KNOWN TO THE ANCIENTS

There are two habitable sectors of the earth's surface, one, in which we live, towards the upper pole, the other towards the other, that is the south pole. These are the only habitable regions; for the lands beyond the tropics are uninhabitable, while the lands beneath the Bear are uninhabitable because of the cold. The facts known to us from journeys by sea and land confirm the conclusion that the length [of our inhabited part of the earth] is much greater than its breadth. For if one reckons up voyages and journeys, so far as they are capable of yielding any accurate information, the distance from the Pillars of Heracles to India exceeds that from Aethiopia to Lake Maeotis and the farthest parts of Scythia by a ratio greater than that of 5 to 3. Yet we know the whole breadth of the habitable world up to the unhabitable regions which bound it, where habitation ceases on the one side because of the cold, on the other because of the heat; while beyond India and the Pillars of Heracles it is the ocean which severs the habitable land and prevents it forming a continuous belt around the globe.

—ARISTOTLE, *Meteorologica* II.5.10–30, adapted from the translation of H. D. P. Lee

144 **cultus, -a, -um**, cultivated (from **colō, colere**, 3, **coluī, cultum**).
  nostrum: genitive of **nōs**.
145 **Caucasus, -ī** (*m*), the Caucasus Mountains between the Black Sea and the Caspian.
  Caucasum hunc . . . illum Gangēn (146): as the elder Scipio speaks, he is pointing
    out these places on the earth. The two points mentioned were located at the
    northeast and southeast extremes of the known world.
  trānscendō, trānscendere (3), **trānscendī, trānscēnsum**, to climb, pass, cross. **trāns-
    cendere . . . trānatāre** (146): personification.
  potuit: the perfect indicative here expresses a potentiality, "could it?"
146 **Gangēs, Gangis** (*m*) (*Greek loan word with Greek acc. ending, -ēn*), the river Ganges.
  trānatō (1), to swim over or across.
  obeō, obīre (*irreg.*), **obīvī** or **obiī, obitum**, to go or come to, go down, (of heavenly
    bodies) set. **obeuntis**: here used for the usual **occidentis**.
147 **auster, austrī** (*m*), the south wind. **amputō** (1), to cut away or off. **Quibus
    amputātīs**: ablative absolute, "Once these (regions) have been cut off (eliminated)."
148 **profectō** (*adv.*), indeed. **quantīs**: what kind of clause does this word introduce?
  *****angustiae, -ārum** (*f pl*), narrowness, want, difficulty. **dīlātō** (1), to extend.
  velit: what form of the verb is this? In what kind of a clause is the verb being used?
149 **quam . . . diū** = **quamdiū**, how long.
150 *****Quīn** (*here used for corroboration and strengthened by* **etiam**), but, indeed, really.
  sī cupiat: what kind of a conditional clause do these words introduce? What mood
    is the main verb of the main clause in this sentence? Why the shift from one
    mood to the other here?
  prōlēs, prōlis (*f*), offspring, descendant, (collective) descendants, posterity.
  deinceps (*adv.*), in a constant series, one after another, successively, in a series.
151 **ūnus quisque**, each one.
152 **ēluviō, ēluviōnis** (*f*), a washing away, overflowing, inundation.
  exustiō, exustiōnis (*f*), a burning up, conflagration.
  ēluviōnēs exustiōnēsque terrārum: "floods and conflagrations." A Stoic doctrine held
    that the earth is periodically doomed to destruction by flood (when the ethereal fires
    are overcome by the moisture in the earth) or by fire (when the fiery element absorbs
    all the moisture); after each of these destructions, the earth is completely renewed.
153 **diūturnus, -a, -um**, of long duration, long lasting.
154 **adsequor, adsequī** (3), **adsecūtus sum**, to reach by pursuing, overtake, gain, obtain.
155 **fore**: future infinitive of **sum**. **nūllus**: supply **sermō**.
  fuerit: what tense of the subjunctive, and why is the subjunctive used here?
157 **ūnīus annī memoriam cōnsequī** (158): "to retain memory of (even) one year."
158 **possit**: why the subjunctive?

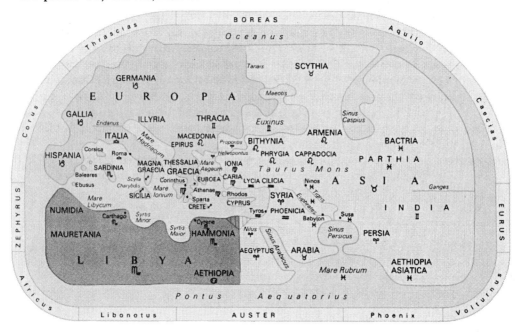

Scipio explains further why any fame gained on this earth must be limited.

144 "Ex hīs ipsīs cultīs nōtīsque terrīs num aut tuum aut cuiusquam nostrum
145 nōmen vel Caucasum hunc, quem cernis, trānscendere potuit vel illum
146 Gangēn trānatāre? Quis in reliquīs orientis aut obeuntis sōlis ultimīs aut
147 aquilōnis austrīve partibus tuum nōmen audiet? Quibus amputātīs cernis
148 profectō quantīs in angustiīs vestra sē glōria dīlātārī velit. Ipsī autem, quī
149 dē nōbīs loquuntur, quam loquentur diū?

1. **What two natural barriers are mentioned as boundaries of the known world and limits to the fame of a Roman?** (145–146) **In what modern countries are they located?**
2. **To what four other parts of the world does the elder Scipio refer?** (146–147)
3. **Why is Scipio's glory unable to spread to those parts of the world?** (147)
4. **How much space is allowed to Scipio's glory?** (148)
5. **In what other way will Scipio's glory be limited?** (148–149)

How far into the future will one's fame last? What about the past?

150 **XXI.** "Quīn etiam, sī cupiat prōlēs illa futūrōrum hominum deinceps
151 laudēs ūnīus cuiusque nostrum ā patribus acceptās posterīs prōdere, tamen
152 propter ēluviōnēs exustiōnēsque terrārum, quās accidere tempore certō
153 necesse est, nōn modo nōn aeternam, sed nē diūturnam quidem glōriam
154 adsequī possumus. Quid autem interest ab iīs quī posteā nāscentur
155 sermōnem fore dē tē, cum ab iīs nūllus fuerit quī ante nātī sunt, [XXII.]
156 quī nec pauciōrēs et certē meliōrēs fuērunt virī; praesertim cum apud eōs
157 ipsōs ā quibus audīrī nōmen nostrum potest, nēmō ūnīus annī memoriam
158 cōnsequī possit?

1. **By what means or in what way is fame preserved?** (150–151)
2. **What is it that the floods and conflagrations will interrupt?** (150–154)
3. **How much time will there be before the next flood or conflagration?** (153–154)
4. **How convincing is the elder Scipio's argument about not being mentioned by those who came before?** (155) **Does it ever bother a person that he has no chance of becoming (or of having been) famous before he was born? Does the final argument here seem to follow naturally from what has been said before, or does it seem to be an afterthought added for rhetorical effect?**
5. **Does the elder Scipio here seem more interested in the temporal extent or in the quality of one's glory or fame?**
6. **In what two ways did men of the past surpass those of the present?** (156) **Why would it have been better to have been known among the men of the past than to be known among those of the present or the future?**
7. **What do you suppose the elder Scipio means by claiming that no one can encompass the recollection of a single year?** (157–158)

(See passages for comparison on page 43)

A map of the world as the ancients imagined it.

41

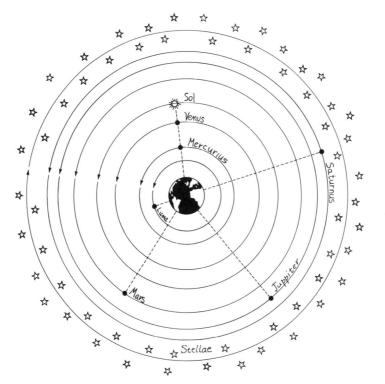

A great part of the earth will be covered over by water when the fated day of the deluge comes. Will it be by the force of the ocean and the rising of the outer sea against us or will heavy rains fall without ceasing and persistent winter eliminate summer and hurl the full force of water down from burst clouds? Or will the earth pour out rivers far and wide and open new springs? Or will there be no single cause for such a catastrophe but rather all principles working together; at the same time the rains will descend, the rivers rise, the seas rush violently from their places, and all things in a united effort will apply themselves to the destruction of the human race? And so it will be. Nothing is difficult for nature, especially when she rushes to destroy herself.

—SENECA, *Naturales quaestiones* III.27.1–2, adapted from the translation of T. H. Corcoran

But the stars are of a fiery substance, and for this reason they are nourished by the vapors of the earth, the sea, and the waters, which are raised up by the sun out of the fields which it warms and out of the waters; and when nourished and renewed by these vapors the stars and the whole aether shed them back again, and then once more draw them up from the same source, with the loss of none of their matter, or only of an extremely small part which is consumed by the fire of the stars and the flame of the aether. As a consequence of this, so our school believes, though it used to be said that Panaetius questioned the doctrine, there will ultimately occur a conflagration of the whole world, because when the moisture has been used up neither can the earth be nourished nor will the air continue to flow, being unable to rise upward after it has drunk up all the water; thus nothing will remain but fire, by which, as a living being and a god, once again a new world may be created and the ordered universe be restored as before.

—CICERO, *De natura deorum* II.XLVI.118, adapted from the translation of H. Rackham

Top left: *Ptolemy is directed in his use of a quadrant by one of the nine Greek Muses, Urania, the patron of astronomy.*

Bottom left: *The solar system according to ancient astronomers.*

159 **populāriter** (*adv.*), after the manner of the common people, commonly, vulgarly.
   tantum modo: = **tantummodo**, only.
   *****astrum, -ī** (*n*), star, constellation, heavenly body, (here) the sun.
160 **mētior, mētīrī** (4), **mēnsus sum**, to measure.
   semel (*adv.*), once, at some time.
161 **dēscrīptiō, dēscrīptiōnis** (*f*), plan, diagram, description. **eandem . . . caelī**
   dēscrīptiōnem: i.e., with the planets in exactly the same positions in which they
   were at the beginning of the "great year."
162 **vertēns**: intransitive here.
163 *****saeculum, -ī** (*n*), generation, lifetime, age, period of a hundred years, century.
   teneantur: why the subjunctive?
164 **ōlim**, once (upon a time).
   *****dēficiō, dēficere** (3), **dēfēcī, dēfectum**, to loosen, set free, desert, fail, (of the sun or
   moon) suffer eclipse.
165 **penetrō** (1), to enter, penetrate.
   quandōque: = **quandōcumque**, at whatever time, whenever. Here with future perfect
   indicative.
166 **iterum** (*adv.*), again.
   signum, -ī (*n*), (here) sign in the heavens, constellation.
   *****prīncipium, -ī** (*n*), beginning.
167 **revocō** (1), to call back.
   expleō, explēre (2), **explēvī, explētum**, to bring to fullness, complete. Supply **esse** to
   make a perfect passive infinitive.
168 **vīcēsimus, -a, -um**, twentieth.
   *****scītō**: future imperative.
   convertō, convertere (3), **convertī, conversum**, to turn or whirl around, complete (a
   period of time) in the course of a revolution. **conversus, -a, -um**, completed.

The elder Scipio describes the "great year."

159 "Hominēs enim populāriter annum tantum modo sōlis, id est unīus astrī,
160 reditū mētiuntur; rē ipsā autem cum ad idem unde semel profecta sunt
161 cūncta astra redierint, eandemque tōtīus caelī dēscrīptiōnem longīs
162 intervallīs rettulerint, tum ille vērē vertēns annus appellārī potest; in quō
163 vix dīcere audeō quam multa hominum saecula teneantur. Namque ut
164 ōlim dēficere sōl hominibus exstinguīque vīsus est, cum Rōmulī animus
165 haec ipsa in templa penetrāvit, quandōque ab eādem parte sōl eōdemque
166 tempore iterum dēfēcerit, tum signīs omnibus ad idem prīncipium
167 stellīsque revocātīs explētum annum habētō; cuius quidem annī nōndum
168 vīcēsimam partem scītō esse conversam.

1. **How do most people measure a year?** (159–160)
2. **How does the elder Scipio measure or define the year that can truly be called the** *vertēns annus* **or "revolving year"?** (160–162)
3. **How many generations of men are included in this "great year"?** (162–163)
4. **Does the "great year" begin at a fixed point in time as do our solar or calendar years? Or is it thought of as beginning any time? How long does it last?** (160–168)
5. **What happened when Romulus died?** (163–165)
6. **Why do you suppose Cicero had the elder Scipio choose the death of Romulus as the starting point of the "great year" in his example?**
7. **Is it easy or difficult to conceive of the length of time involved in a "great year"?** (162–163 and 167–168) **What significance could be attributed to the lifetime of an individual man and the span of human memory in comparison with the length of a "great year"?**

THE *MAGNUS ANNUS*

Most marvelous are the motions of the five stars, falsely called planets or wandering stars—for a thing cannot be said to wander if it preserves for all eternity fixed and regular motions, forward, backward, and in other directions. And this regularity is all the more marvelous in the case of the stars we speak of, because at one time they are hidden and at another they are uncovered again; now they approach, now retire; now precede, now follow; now move faster, now slower, now do not move at all but remain for a time stationary. On the diverse motions of the planets the mathematicians have based what they call the Great Year, which is completed when the sun, moon, and five planets having all finished their courses have returned to the same positions relative to one another. The length of this period is hotly debated, but it must necessarily be a fixed and definite time.

—CICERO, *De natura deorum* II.XX.51–52, adapted from the translation of H. Rackham

169 **quōcircā**, for which reason, wherefore.
    omnia: "all things," i.e., "their rewards."
170 **praestāns, praestantis**, preeminent, superior, distinguished, extraordinary.
    quantī: "of how little value."
    tandem, really, after all.
    ista: used contemptuously here.
172 **contueor, contuērī** (2), **contuitus sum**, to look upon, gaze at.
    neque . . . dēdideris (173) **nec . . . posueris**: perfect subjunctives of prohibition with
        neque . . . nec (173) rather than the usual **nē . . . neve**.
174 **oportet**: followed by **trahat**, "it is necessary (that) virtue herself draw you. . . ."
    inlecebra, -ae (f), enticement, attraction, charm, allurement.
    *decus, decoris** (n), splendor, glory, honor.
175 **ipsī videant**: "let them see to it," "let it be their affair." What kind of subjunctive is
    this?
176 **et . . . et** (177) **. . . et**: "both . . . and . . . and."
    cingō, cingere (3), **cinxī, cinctum**, to surround, encircle, enclose.
177 **perennis, -is, -e**, lasting the year through (**per** + **annus**), everlasting.
    obruō, obruere (3), **obruī, obrutum**, to overwhelm, bury, destroy, obliterate. **obruitur**
        . . . extinguitur (178): note the chiastic arrangement of the words between these
        verbs.
    interitus, -ūs (m), destruction, annihilation, death.
    oblīviō, oblīviōnis (f), forgetfulness.
    posteritās, posteritātis (f), posterity.

The elder Scipio urges the younger to contemplate his eternal home in the heavens.

169 **XXIII.** "Quōcircā sī reditum in hunc locum dēspērāveris, in quō omnia
170 sunt magnīs et praestantibus virīs, quantī tandem est ista hominum glōria
171 quae pertinēre vix ad unīus annī partem exiguam potest? Igitur altē
172 spectāre sī volēs atque hanc sēdem et aeternam domum contuērī, neque tē
173 sermōnibus vulgī dēdideris nec in praemiīs hūmānīs spem posueris rērum
174 tuārum; suīs tē oportet inlecebrīs ipsa virtūs trahat ad vērum decus; quid
175 dē tē aliī loquantur ipsī videant, sed loquentur tamen. Sermō autem omnis
176 ille et angustiīs cingitur hīs regiōnum quās vidēs, nec umquam dē ūllō
177 perennis fuit, et obruitur hominum interitū, et oblīviōne posteritātis
178 extinguitur."

1. How long will glory or fame last among men? (170–171)
2. What does the elder Scipio suggest that the younger Scipio contemplate? (171–172) To what had the younger Scipio kept turning his eyes earlier? (123–124)
3. In what should the younger Scipio not put his hope? (172–174)
4. What is it that should lead or motivate him instead? (174)
5. What might virtue's "own attractions" (*suīs . . . inlecebrīs*, 174) be?
6. What should the younger Scipio's attitude be toward what other men say? (174–175)
7. Where are the things that other men say confined, and what happens to them? (175–178)
8. Summarize the arguments that the elder Scipio has been making in trying to attract the younger Scipio away from a search for earthly glory and to higher goals.

This antique double exposure is a page from one of the most famous of palimpsest ("rescraped") manuscripts. During the Dark Ages it was a common practice to scrape the writing from unread books and use the valuable parchment over again. But the ghost of the old text often lingered beneath the new, waiting to be discovered by the scholars of a later age (nowadays aided by chemicals and infrared photographs). In this case a fifth or sixth century manuscript of Cicero's De republica (double columns) was found to underlie a late seventh-century copy of a work by Saint Augustine. Until the Vatican librarian Angelo Mai recovered it from these pages in 1820, the Cicero was known only in fragmentary form. The "Somnium Scipionis," however, although it was a part of the De republica, was known independently throughout the Middle Ages.

179 **síquidem**, if indeed, if it is really true that.
180 **mereor, merērī** (2), **meritus sum**, to deserve, merit, be entitled to, be worthy of.
    bene merērī dē aliquā rē: lit., "to deserve well from something" = "to behave
    well toward it." **bene** (179) **meritīs dē patriā**: "those who have deserved well of the
    fatherland" or "those who have behaved well toward the fatherland" = "good
    citizens."
    līmes, līmitis (*m*), path, road, way.
    quamquam, although.
    pueritia, -ae (*f*), boyhood, youth.
181 **ingredior, ingredī** (3), **ingressus sum** (+ *dat.*), to trod in or on.
182 **ēnītor, ēnītī** (3), **ēnīsus sum**, to exert oneself, make an effort, struggle, strive.
    vigilantius (*comparative adverb*), more watchfully, carefully, vigilantly.
    ēnītēre: present imperative of **ēnītor** (see above, note to line 182).
185 **digitus, -ī** (*m*), finger.
186 **vigeō, vigēre** (2), **viguī**, to be lively or vigorous, thrive, flourish.
    tam . . . quam (187), just as.
    moderor, moderārī (1), **moderātus sum**, to set a measure or limit to a thing, moder-
    ate, restrain, regulate, guide, govern.
187 **cui**: dative with **praepositus est**; the antecedent is **corpus.**
    praepōnō, praepōnere (3), **praeposuī, praepositum** (+ *dat.*), to put or set before, place
    over as chief or commander.
188 **ex quādam parte mortālem**: "partly mortal."
189 **fragilis, -is, -e** (*from* **frangō, frangere**, 3, **frēgī, fractum**, to break), easily broken, frag-
    ile, perishable. **fragile corpus animus sempiternus**: chiasmus.

KNOW THAT YOU ARE GOD

But what do we understand by divine attributes? Activity, wisdom,
discovery, memory (**vigēre, sapere, invenīre, meminisse**). Therefore the
soul is, as I say, divine, as Euripides dares to say, God: and in fact, if
God is either air or fire, so also is the soul of man; for just as the
heavenly nature is free from earth and moisture, so the human soul is
without trace of either element. For in these elements there is nothing
to possess the power of memory, thought, reflection, nothing capable
of retaining the past; or foreseeing the future and grasping the present,
and these capacities are nothing but divine; and never will there be
found any source from which they can come to men except from God.
There is then a peculiar essential character belonging to the soul, distinct from these common and well-known elements. Accordingly,
whatever it is that is conscious, that is wise, that lives, that is active
must be heavenly and divine and for that reason eternal.

—CICERO, *Tusculanae disputationes* I.XXVI.65–XXVII.66, adapted from the
translation of J. E. King

Encouraged by the prospect of access to heaven, the younger Scipio renews his commitment of dedication to his country.

179 **XXIV.** Quae cum dīxisset, "Ego vērō," inquam, "Āfricāne, sīquidem bene
180 meritīs dē patriā quasi līmes ad caelī aditum patet, quamquam ā pueritiā
181 vestīgiīs ingressus patris et tuīs decorī vestrō nōn dēfuī, nunc tamen tantō
182 praemiō expositō ēnītar multō vigilantius." Et ille, "Tū vērō ēnītere et sīc
183 habētō, nōn esse tē mortālem, sed corpus hoc; nec enim tū is es quem
184 fōrma ista dēclārat, sed mēns cuiusque is est quisque, nōn ea figūra quae
185 digitō dēmōnstrārī potest. Deum tē igitur scītō esse, sīquidem est deus quī
186 viget, quī sentit, quī meminit, quī prōvidet, quī tam regit et moderātur et
187 movet id corpus cui praepositus est quam hunc mundum ille prīnceps
188 deus; et ut mundum ex quādam parte mortālem ipse deus aeternus, sīc
189 fragile corpus animus sempiternus movet.

1. **Judging from the younger Scipio's reply, what effect have the elder Scipio's discourse and exhortations had on him?** (179–182)
2. **For what people does the pathway to heaven lie open?** (179–180)
3. **What does the younger Scipio say of his former efforts at emulating his father and his adoptive grandfather?** (180–181) **What does he promise in the way of future efforts?** (181–182)
4. **What does the elder Scipio say about the physical form of man, which can be pointed out by the finger? What is the real man?** (182–185)
5. **How is the mind of man like god? What are the functions of god as described by the elder Scipio?** (185–189)
6. **How are man's body and the world alike?** (188–189)

YOU ARE NOT YOUR BODY

When I study the nature of the soul, the conception of it in the body, as it were in a home that is not its own, presents itself as one much more difficult, much more doubtful than the conception of the nature of the soul when it has quitted the body and come into the free heaven, as it were to its home. It is a point of the utmost importance to realize that the soul sees by means of the soul alone, and surely this is the meaning of Apollo's maxim advising that each one should know himself. For I do not suppose the meaning of the maxim is that we should know our limbs, our height, or our shape; our selves are not bodies, and in speaking as I do to you, I am not speaking to your body. When Apollo says, "Know thyself," he says, "Know thy soul." For the body is as it were a vessel or a sort of shelter for the soul.

—CICERO, *Tusculanae disputationes* I.XXII.51–52, adapted from the translation of J. E. King

191 ***agitō** (1), to put a thing in motion, drive, impel, move.
*aliunde (*adv.*), from another place, person, or thing.
192 **habeat**: subjunctive dependent on **necesse est.**
193 **dēsinō, dēsinere** (3), **dēsiī, desitum**, to leave off, cease, desist, stop, end.
quīn etiam, indeed, in fact.
194 **hic . . . hoc**: subject pronouns referring to the neuter **quod sēsē movet** (192) and
attracted into the gender of the predicate nouns **fōns** and **prīncipium.**
fōns, fontis (*m*), spring, fountain, source, origin, cause.
195 **orīgō, orīginis** (*f*), earliest beginning, source, origin.
196 **quod**: the relative pronoun has conditional force here in a present contrary-to-fact
statement; translate "if it. . . ."
197 **gignō, gignere** (3), **genuī, genitum**, to beget, bring forth, bear, produce, (passive) be
born, spring, arise, proceed. **quodsī**, but if.
occidō, occidere (3), **occidī, occāsum**, to fall, die, pass away. **oritur . . . occidit**: "is
born . . . perishes"; these words are often used of the rising and setting of heavenly bodies.
198 **extinctum**: the participle is used here with the force of a conditional clause.
renāscor, renāscī (3), **renātus sum**, to be born again, rise or spring up again.
199 **creō** (1), to create.
200 **sit**: subjunctive in a substantive clause of result after **fit.**
201 **vel**, or else. **concidō, concidere** (3), **concidī**, to fall together, fall down. The subjunctives **concidat, cōnsistat**, and **nancīscātur** (202) depend on **necesse est** (201–
202). **et . . . nec** (202): and . . . and . . . not.
202 **quā**: "by which"; the antecedent is **vim ūllam**, and the relative pronoun introduces
a clause of purpose.
ā prīmō, from the beginning, (here) again.
impellō, impellere (3), **impulī, impulsum**, to push, drive, or strike against, drive
forward, set in motion. **impulsa**: supply **nātūra** from earlier in the sentence.
impulsa moveātur: "be impelled and set in motion."

A portrait bust of Cicero.

Africanus describes the "first cause" of all motion and explains why it must be eternal.

190 **XXV.** "Nam quod semper movētur, aeternum est; quod autem mōtum
191 adfert alicui quodque ipsum agitātur aliunde, quandō fīnem habet mōtūs,
192 vīvendī fīnem habeat necesse est. Sōlum igitur quod sēsē movet, quia
193 numquam dēseritur ā sē, numquam nē movērī quidem dēsinit; quīn etiam
194 cēterīs, quae moventur, hic fōns, hoc prīncipium est movendī. Prīncipiī
195 autem nūlla est orīgō; nam ex prīncipiō oriuntur omnia, ipsum autem
196 nūllā ex rē aliā nascī potest; nec enim esset id prīncipium, quod
197 gignerētur aliunde; quodsī numquam oritur, nec occidit quidem umquam.
198 Nam prīncipium extinctum nec ipsum ab aliō renāscētur nec ex sē aliud
199 creābit, sīquidem necesse est ā prīncipiō orīrī omnia. Ita fit ut mōtūs
200 prīncipium ex eō sit quod ipsum ā sē movētur; id autem nec nāscī potest
201 nec morī; vel concidat omne caelum omnisque nātūra et cōnsistat necesse
202 est nec vim ūllam nancīscātur quā ā prīmō impulsa moveātur.

1. **What is eternal? How is it defined?** (190)
2. **What is mortal? How is it defined?** (190–192)
3. **How is the first cause, the source of motion in all other things, defined?** (192–194)
4. **Why can the first cause itself have no beginning or end?** (194–197)
5. **What would happen if the first cause were extinguished?** (198–199)
6. **How is the continued life of the world dependent on the first cause?** (199–202)
7. **Does repetition of words in this passage strengthen or weaken the force of Scipio's argument?**
8. **Why do you think Cicero chose to put such a literal translation of Plato into the elder Scipio's mouth?**

CICERO TRANSLATED THE PASSAGE ABOVE AND ITS CONTINUATION ON PAGE 53 FROM A FAMOUS PASSAGE IN PLATO'S *PHAEDRUS* (245), WHICH IS GIVEN HERE IN THE TRANSLATION OF B. JOWETT:

The soul through all her being is immortal, for that which is ever in motion is immortal; but that which moves another and is moved by another, in ceasing to move ceases also to live. Only the self-moving, never leaving self, never ceases to move, and is the fountain and beginning of motion to all that moves besides. Now, the beginning is unbegotten, for that which is begotten has a beginning; but the beginning is begotten of nothing, for if it were begotten of something, then the begotten would not come from a beginning. But if unbegotten, it must also be indestructible; for if beginning were destroyed, there could be no beginning out of anything, nor anything out of a beginning; and all things must have a beginning. And therefore the self-moving is the beginning of motion; and this can neither be destroyed nor begotten, else the whole heavens and all creation would collapse and stand still, and never again have motion or birth.

(continued)

203 **Cum pateat**: causal clause with the subjunctive.
    quod . . . moveātur: subjunctive in a relative clause within an indirect statement.
204 **hanc nātūram**: i.e., this property of being self-moving. **neget**: subjunctive in a relative clause of characteristic. **inanimus, -a, -um**, lifeless, inanimate, without spirit.
205 **pulsus, -ūs** (*m*), a pushing, striking, blow.
    externus, -a, -um, outward, external, foreign.
    animal, animālis (*n*), animal. Here the noun is used as an equivalent of the adjective **animālis, -is, -e**, animate, living, with spirit.
206 **cieō, ciēre** (2), **cīvī, citum**, to move, set in motion.
    proprius, -a, -um, one's or its own, special, particular, proper.
    quae sī (207) **est ūna ex omnibus. . . .**: "and if it is this one force out of all that itself moves itself. . . ."
207 **quae sē ipsa moveat**: relative clause of characteristic.
    neque . . . et: "it is both not . . ., and it is. . . ."
    nātus, -a, -um, born, produced by birth.

This mosaic represents a gathering of scholars, philosophers, or statesmen such as the one at Scipio's villa when he relates his dream.

The soul is moved by itself and not from without, and so it must be immortal.

203 **XXVI.** "Cum pateat igitur aeternum id esse quod ā sē ipsō moveātur,
204 quis est quī hanc nātūram animīs esse tribūtam neget? Inanimum est
205 enim omne quod pulsū agitātur externō; quod autem est animal, id mōtū
206 ciētur interiōre et suō; nam haec est propria nātūra animī atque vīs; quae
207 sī est ūna ex omnibus quae sē ipsa moveat, neque nāta certē est et aeterna
208 est.

1. What is the demonstration of the nature of the first cause in the previous passage used to prove in this passage? (203–204)
2. What, according to the elder Scipio, is the essential difference between something that is inanimate and something that is animate? (204–206)
3. What is the essential nature of the spirit or soul, according to the elder Scipio? (206–207)
4. What is the final thing that the elder Scipio seeks to prove here about the soul? (207–208)

CONTINUATION OF THE PASSAGE FROM PLATO'S *PHAEDRUS*:

But if the self-moving is proved to be immortal, he who affirms that self-motion is the very idea and essence of the soul will not be put to confusion. For the body which is moved from without is soulless; but that which is moved from within has a soul, for such is the nature of the soul. But if this be true, must not the soul be the self-moving, and therefore of necessity unbegotten and immortal?

The fourth century B.C. Greek philosopher Plato, whose work Cicero knew well and admired. His work **The Republic** *was the inspiration for Cicero's* De republica.

209 **Hanc**: to what in the previous paragraph does this word refer?
210 **exercitō** (1), to exercise, practice. **exercitātus, -a, -um**, well-exercised, practiced, versed, trained. **vēlōcius**, more swiftly.
211 **pervolō** (1), to fly to. **ōcius**, more swiftly. **iam tum, cum**, while still.
212 **inclūdō, inclūdere** (3), **inclūsī, inclūsum**, to shut in, confine, enclose, imprison. **ēmineō, ēminēre** (2), **ēminuī**, to stand out, project. **forās** (adv.), out through the doors, out-of-doors, forth.
213 **abstrahō, abstrahere** (3), **abstraxī, abstractum**, to draw, pull, drag away. **quī**: subject of **dēdidērunt** (214), **praebuērunt**, and **violāvērunt** (216).
214 ***voluptās, voluptātis** (f), satisfaction, enjoyment, pleasure, delight. **minister, ministrī** (m), attendant, waiter, servant.
215 **impulsus, -ūs** (m), a pushing or striking against, impulse, blow. **libīdō, libīdinis** (f), pleasure, desire, passion. **oboediēns, oboedientis** (+ dat.), obedient, compliant.
216 **violō** (1), to injure, dishonor, outrage, violate. **corporibus**: ablative of separation with **ēlāpsī**. **ēlābor, ēlābī** (3), **ēlāpsus sum**, to slip or glide away, escape from (+ ablative of separation). **volūtō** (1), to roll, turn, twist about. Passive in reflexive sense: "they roll themselves," "they roll."
217 **exagitō** (1), to stir up, disturb, harass, persecute, torment.
218 **solvō, solvere** (3), **solvī, solūtum**, to set free, release.

That soul, I say, herself invisible, departs to the invisible world—to the divine and immortal and rational; thither arriving, she is secure of bliss and is released from the error and folly of men, their fears and wild passions and all other human ills, and for ever dwells, as they say of the initiated, in company with the gods.

—PLATO, *Phaedo* 80–81, translated by B. Jowett

PLATO'S DESCRIPTION OF THE FATE OF SOULS THAT HAVE DEVOTED THEMSELVES TO PLEASURE

But the soul that has been polluted, and is impure at the time of her departure, and is the companion and servant of the body always, and is in love with and fascinated by the body and by the desires and pleasures of the body, the soul, I mean, accustomed to hate and fear and avoid the intellectual principle;—do you suppose that such a soul will depart pure and unalloyed? She is held fast by the corporeal, which the continual association and constant care of the body have wrought into her nature. And this corporeal element is heavy and weighty and earthy, and is that element of sight by which a soul is depressed and dragged down again into the visible world—prowling about tombs and sepulchres, near which, as they tell us, are seen certain ghostly apparitions of souls which have not departed pure, but are cloyed with sight and therefore visible. These souls are compelled to wander about such places in payment of the penalty of their former evil way of life; and they continue to wander until through the craving after the corporeal which never leaves them, they are imprisoned finally in another body. And they may be supposed to find their prisons in the same natures which they have had in their former lives.

—PLATO, *Phaedo* 81, adapted from the translation of B. Jowett

Souls that devote themselves to patriotic pursuits and contemplate higher things will return more swiftly to their heavenly homes.

209   "Hanc tū exerce in optimīs rēbus! Sunt autem optimae cūrae dē salūte
210 patriae, quibus agitātus et exercitātus animus vēlōcius in hanc sēdem et
211 domum suam pervolābit; idque ōcius faciet, sī iam tum, cum erit
212 inclūsus in corpore, ēminēbit forās et ea quae extrā erunt contemplāns
213 quam maximē sē ā corpore abstrahet. Namque eōrum animī quī sē
214 corporis voluptātibus dēdidērunt eārumque sē quasi ministrōs praebuērunt
215 impulsūque libīdinum voluptātibus oboedientium deōrum et hominum
216 iūra violāvērunt, corporibus ēlāpsī circum terram ipsam volūtantur nec
217 hunc in locum nisi multīs exagitātī saeculīs revertuntur."
218   Ille discessit; ego somnō solūtus sum.

1. **What does the elder Scipio regard as the "best pursuits" (*optimīs rēbus*) for the soul? (209–210)**
2. **How would these pursuits differ from the pursuit of individual glory?**
3. **What activity beside exercise of concern for the safety of one's country will enable the soul to fly to its home more rapidly? (211–213)**
4. **What things do you think the elder Scipio would want the soul to contemplate? (212)**
5. **How would contemplation of these things tend to draw the soul away from the body? (212–213)**
6. **Do you think that the elder Scipio sees a necessary connection between abandoning oneself to pleasures and violation of the laws of men and gods? (213–216) Do you think it is possible to indulge in pleasures without ending up violating the laws of men and gods? Explain your answers to these questions and cite examples from real life (ancient and modern).**
7. **What philosophical school is Cicero indirectly condemning here? (215)**
8. **Can you see any connection between abandonment of oneself to pleasures and the quest for earthly glory earlier in the work? Is the enjoyment of earthly glory a pleasure? To what does the elder Scipio wish to direct the younger Scipio's attention instead?**
9. **What happens to the souls of the pleasure-loving? When do they finally return to their home in the heavens? (216–217)**
10. **In the beginning of this work the younger Scipio says he was "embraced" by a deep sleep (16). In what terms does he describe his awakening?**
11. **Does the last line provide a satisfactory conclusion for the work? If so, how?**

PLATO'S DESCRIPTION OF THE FATE OF SOULS THAT HAVE DEVOTED THEMSELVES TO PHILOSOPHY

The soul which is pure at departing and draws after her no bodily taint, having never voluntarily during life had connection with the body, which she is ever avoiding, herself gathered into herself;—and making such abstraction her perpetual study—which means that she has been a true disciple of philosophy; and therefore has in fact been always engaged in the practice of dying? For is not philosophy the study of death?—

    Certainly—

(*continued* on page 54.)

PASSAGES FOR COMPARISON

PLATO, THE *REPUBLIC*

At the end of the tenth and last book of Plato's *Republic*, written in the fourth century B.C., occurs the famous myth of Er, which gave Cicero the idea for including the dream of Scipio at the end of his *De republica*. The translation of the myth of Er given below is that of I. A. Richards. After reading it, answer the following questions:

1. In what way is the experience of Er similar to a dream (such as that in the "Somnium Scipionis")?
2. Compare the journey of the soul as reported by Er to the journey of the soul described in the "Somnium Scipionis."
3. How is the conception of the universe in the Platonic passage similar to that in Cicero? How is it. different?
4. What, according to Er, is most important for the individual human soul?
5. What kinds of political figures are described in Er's report? Compare them with the political figures mentioned in the "Somnium Scipionis."
6. What is the moral that is extracted from Er's report at the end? How is it similar to or different from the moral of the "Somnium Scipionis"?
7. Which is more concrete and historical, the "Somnium Scipionis" or the tale told by Er? Which is more abstract and general?
8. Is the individual or the state more important in the myth of Er? Which is more important in the "Somnium Scipionis"?
9. Which do you find more appealing, the "Somnium Scipionis" or the myth of Er? Why?
10. Which seems to you to be more relevant to contemporary political, social, and moral issues, the "Somnium Scipionis" or the myth of Er? Why?

This is not the story Alcinous heard, but the story of a brave man, Er, the son of Armenius, a Pamphylian by birth. It came about that, after falling in the fight, his body was taken up on the tenth day, unchanged, and on the twelfth day when his body was stretched on the wood ready to be burned, he came back to life, and he gave this account of what he had seen over there on the other side. He said that when his soul went out of his body, he journeyed in company with a great band of others till they came to a strange place, where two openings side by side in the earth faced two others in the heavens. Between them were judges who fixed on the just a sign of their reward in front and on the backs of the unjust an account of their crimes, and the just they sent up through the heaven on the right hand and the unjust down by the lower way on the left. When Er came before them himself, they said that he was to be a witness to men to report to them of that other world, and they ordered him to watch and hear

56

everything in that place. Then he saw the souls after judgement going off by one of the openings of heaven and one of earth, while by the other two openings other souls were coming back, dirty and covered with dust from under earth, or clean and shining from heaven. They kept coming back as if from a long journey, and gladly took up their places on the field as persons do at some great festival. Friends welcomed one another, and those from within the earth asked about the heaven, and in turn were questioned about the life under earth. And these wept and cried out at the memory of all the things they had seen and undergone in their journey down under the earth—it went on a thousand years—while those from heaven talked of joys and visions of things more beautiful than any words might picture. The full story, Glaucon, would take us overlong, but this, Er said, was the substance. For every wrong they had done to others, they made a payment ten times as great; and this was measured in periods of a hundred years, for a human life was taken to be a hundred years long, so that they had ten punishments for every crime; and again those who had done good acts, and had been just and holy men, would get their reward in the same measure. And other things not to be recorded he said of those new born who lived a short time only. And there were rewards and punishments still greater for those who were pious or impious to their parents or to the gods, or who put themselves to death. He was within hearing when one was questioned by another, "Where is Ardiaeos the Great?" Now this Ardiaeos had been ruler in a town of Pamphylia a thousand years before that time, and had put to death his old father and a brother older than himself, and had done numbers of other unholy things. And the other answered, "He has not come, and probably will never come. For this was one of the fearful things we saw. When we were near the mouth, and were about to come out, and all our pains were ended, we suddenly saw him with others, most of them tyrants, though some were private persons who had done great wrongs. And when these were about to go up and out, the mouth would not take them, but roared when any of those who were too evil to be reformed, or who had not completed their punishment, attempted to come up. "And then," he said, "violent men, like fire to look at, who heard the Voice, would seize them and take them off; and Ardiaeos and others they took and knotted with cords, head and hand and foot, and dragged them by the wayside, combing them with thorns, like wool, and saying to those who went by why this was and that they were to be thrown into Tartarus." And then, of all they had undergone this fear was the worst for each—that the mouth would roar when he attempted to go up, and everyone went up most gladly when the Voice was quiet. These, said Er, were among the pains and punishments, and there were rewards as great.

Now when they had been in the green field seven days, they were forced to journey on, and they came in four days to a place where they saw, stretching from on high through the heaven and the earth, a straight line like a pillar, and like the rainbow, but brighter and clearer. They came to this after another day's journey, and there at the middle of the light they saw the ends of its chain stretching from heaven; for this light was the band which keeps the heavens together, like the bands about a ship. And from the ends was stretched the spindle of Necessity, on which all the circles turn. Its rod and hook were made of steel, and the whorl upon it was made of steel and other materials. And the form of the whorl was like those used on the earth: from his account there seems to be one great hollow whorl, and another within it, like boxes which go inside one another, and in the same way a third, a fourth, and four others, for there were eight of the whorls in all, one within another, their edges seeming like circles from the upper side but together they form the back of one solid whorl about the rod, which is fixed right through the middle of the eighth. The first and outermost whorl has the widest edge, the sixth has the second widest, then the fourth, then the eighth, then the seventh, then the fifth, then the third, and the second has the narrowest edge. The edge of the greatest whorl is of mixed colors; that of the seventh is brightest; that of the eighth takes its color from the seventh shining upon it. The colors of the second and fifth are like one another, being warmer than the seventh and eighth. The third is whitest, the fourth is a little red, and the sixth is the second whitest. The whole spindle turns one way, but within the unit as it turns the seven inner circles turn gently in the opposite direction, and of these seven the eighth moves most quickly, and after it the seventh, sixth, and fifth move together, and more slowly turns the fourth as it seemed, moving back upon itself, and then the third, and the fifth and slowest motion is that of the second. And the spindle turns round upon the knees of Necessity. On every one of its circles is a Siren, who travels round with the circle, and cries out on one note, and the eight notes are joined in one harmony. And round about are seated at equal distances the Fates, the daughters of Necessity, Lachesis, Clotho and Atropos; who, clothed in white robes, with flowers on their heads, keep harmony in their song with the music of the Sirens. And the song of Lachesis is of the past; that of Clotho, of the present; that of Atropos, of the future. And Clotho with her right hand helps to turn the outer edge of the whorl, stopping from time to time, and Atropos with her left hand turns the inner circles, while Lachesis in turn helps one or the other.

Now, coming here, the souls were sent at once before Lachesis, and first a sort of prophet placed them in order, and having taken from the knees of Lachesis certain lots and designs of lives, went up to a high pulpit and said, "The word of Lachesis, daughter of Necessity: Souls that live for a day, here is the start of another round taking men back to death. Your daimon will not be given you by chance but will be of your own choosing. Let him who gets the first lot choose the life he wills, which then shall be his destiny. But Virtue is free; a man will have more or less of her, as he honors her or not. He who chooses is responsible, Heaven is guiltless." Having said this, he cast the lots down among them all, and every soul took up the lot that fell to him, all but Er, who was ordered not to do so. After this the prophet placed designs of lives before them on the earth, and they were far greater in number than the company. They were of every sort, for there were lives of all sorts of animals and all sorts of men, there were tyrannies among them, some unbroken till the end, and others cut short and changing into poverty, beggardom and exile. And there were lives of men noted for their beautiful forms and faces and strength as athletes, or for their high birth and the virtues of their fathers, and lives of the opposite sorts; and of women the same. But quality of soul was not fixed in them, because a soul taking up a different life necessarily becomes different. But all the other things were mixed with one another, and with riches and poverty, disease and strength, and the middle ways between them.

There, my dear Glaucon is the danger of dangers for every man. That is why every one of us—putting all other cares on one side—has to look for the man who will give him the power and the knowledge to separate the life which is good from that which is bad, and always and everywhere to make the best decision which conditions offer him. And let him take into account all the things we have talked of, and see how the quality of his life will be changed by their being present or not present in it. Let him judge the effects of high and low birth, private station and office, of being strong or feeble, quick or slow, and all such gifts of the soul, natural or gained by experience, when mixed and joined with one another; so that by weighing all these things he will be able to make a reasonable decision between the better and the worse life, with his eyes fixed on the innermost being of the soul, naming as the worst life that which will have a tendency to make it more unjust, and the better that which will make it more just. But all other thoughts he will let be, for we have seen that this is the best decision, for life and for death. A man needs to take with him to the house of death an adamantine faith in this, so that even there he may not be dazzled by wealth and other frippery, and jump into tyrannies and such like crimes, and so do evil which can never be put right, and undergo still greater himself; but may always be able to judge and take the life which is in the middle way, and keep from excess in this direction or that, in this life so far as may be and in the life to come; for this is man's greatest happiness.

Moreover, the witness from the other side reported that the prophet then said: "Even he who comes forward last, if he chooses wisely, and lives hard and seriously, will get a good enough life, not an evil one. Let not the first make his choice without care, or the last be down-hearted." When the prophet had said these things, the one who had the first number jumped at once for the greatest tyranny, and in his foolish greed he took it without examination, not seeing that he was fated by it to eat his own children, and other shocking things. And when he looked it over, he hammered his breast and lamented over his choice, without recalling what the prophet had said. He did not look upon himself as responsible, but cried out against chance and the gods and anything but himself. He was one of those who had come down from heaven, a man who had lived in a well-ordered government, and so had gained some measure of virtue by use, and not by philosophy. It seems that of those who were thus overtaken, not a few came from heaven; they had not been schooled by trouble. For most of those who came from under earth did not choose carelessly, for they had undergone pain themselves, and had seen the pain of others. For which reason as well as through the chances in the lots there was generally an exchange of the good and bad. But if whenever he comes back to the life of this earth, a man loves wisdom and does not get one of the very last numbers, by this report he will not only be happy here, but his journey back to this world will not be rough and under the earth, but smooth and through the heavens. Passing strange as it was, he said, how the different souls chose their lives—sad and absurd, and foolish, for their choice was guided for the most part by what they were used to in their earlier lives. He saw the soul of Orpheus, he said, choose the life of a swan, for he hated all women because of his death at their hands, and was unwilling to have a woman give him birth. He saw the soul of Thamyris choosing the life of a nightingale, and a swan changing over to the life of a man, and the same with other music-making animals. The soul which had the twentieth number took the life of a lion; it was the soul of Ajax, the son of Telamon, which, remembering the decision as to the arms of Achilles, was unwilling to become a man. The one after, the soul of Agamemnon, for the same reason that its pains had made it hate all men, changed to the life of an eagle. The soul of Atalanta gave one look at the great honors of an athlete's life and grasped them at once, unable to go farther. After her, he said, he saw the soul of Epeius, the son of Panopeus, taking on the nature of an expert work-woman. Far off at the back the soul of the clown Thersites was putting on the body of an ape. And it chanced that the soul of Odysseus had the last number of all, and came to make its selection. From memory of the toils of its last life, it had no longer any ambition, and went about everywhere in search of the quiet life of a private person, and was a long time looking till it saw it at last in some out-of-the-way place untouched by the others, and, on seeing it, said that it would have done the same if it had had the first number, and took it gladly. And in the same way with the rest: beasts changed into men and into one another, the unjust into cruel beasts, the just to gentle ones, and there were mixtures of all sorts. But now, when all the souls had chosen lives in the order of their numbers, they were taken in turn before Lachesis. And she sent with every one the daimon he had chosen to guide his life and see that all came true. And this guide first took the soul to Clotho, under the twisting motion of her hand, and so fixed the destiny he had chosen. After touching her, the daimon took the soul to the turning hand of Atropos, that the threads might never be untwisted. From there, the souls traveled without turning back under the throne of Necessity. When all had passed, they journeyed into the Levels of Oblivion, through thick, painful heat, for there were no trees or plants; and in the evening they stopped by the River of Unmindfulness whose water no vessel may keep. They were all made to take a measure of the water; those who were not saved by their good sense drank more than the measure, so that all memory of everything went from them. And after they had gone to sleep and it was the middle of the night, there was a sound of thunder and a shaking of the earth, and they were suddenly sent away, one this way, one that, up to their birth, like quickly moving stars. Er himself, he said, was kept from drinking the water; but he had no idea how and in what way he went back to his body. Only he suddenly opened his eyes at dawn, and saw himself stretched on a funeral pyre.

And so, Glaucon, the story was saved, and will save us, if we believe it; we will pass safely across the River of Lethe, and keep our souls clean. If you will be guided by me, we will believe that the soul lives forever, and is able to undergo every measure of good and evil. We will keep ever to the upward road, and follow justice and reason always and in every way, that we may be friends to ourselves and to the gods, both while we are here and when, like victors in the games, we have our reward. And so, here on earth and in that journey of a thousand years, it will be well with us.

LUCRETIUS, *DE RERUM NATURA*

Much of the speculation about the nature of the universe and the destiny of the human soul in Cicero's "Somnium Scipionis" may be traced back to Stoic philosophy and beyond that to Plato and the Pythagorean tradition. Starkly opposed to all of this were the philosophical views of Cicero's contemporary, the great didactic poet Lucretius (ca. 94–55 B.C.), who was an adherent and exponent of the philosophy of Epicurus (mid-fourth to early third century B.C.), which in turn was based on the atomistic theories of Democritus (late fifth century B.C.). In contrast to the Stoics' insistence on self-discipline and duty, the Epicureans taught the desirability of sensible enjoyment of personal pleasures. Lucretius describes the Epicurean ideal by describing how groups of men, "stretched forth . . . upon the soft grass beside a rill of water under the branches of a tall tree, . . . merrily refresh themselves at no great cost, especially when the weather smiles, and the season of the year besprinkles the green herbage with flowers" (*De rerum natura* II.29–33, tr. by W. H. D. Rouse and M. F. Smith). Lucretius died about 55 B.C., leaving his didactic epic poem on the nature of things, the *De rerum natura*, unfinished. Cicero, early in 54 B.C., the very year in which he began work on his *De republica*, wrote about Lucretius' poem in a letter to his brother (*ad Quintum fratrem* II.11.5) and praised the artistry of the poem. Nothing, however, could be farther removed from the views that Cicero expounds in the *De republica* and the "Somnium Scipionis" than the philosophy of Lucretius and the Epicureans.

While the "Somnium" is premised on the belief that the soul is divine and immortal, Lucretius regarded it as physical and subject to death along with the body. Lucretius argued this point at great length in the third book of his poem in a passage that begins as follows (III.417–462, tr. by W. H. D. Rouse and M. F. Smith):

Listen now: that you may be able to recognize that the minds and light spirits of living creatures are born and are mortal, I shall proceed to set forth verses worthy of your character, long sought out and found with delightful toil. Be so good as to apply both these names to one thing; and when for example I speak of spirit, showing it to be mortal, believe me to speak also of mind, inasmuch as it is one thing and a combined nature.

First of all, since I have shown it to be delicate and composed of minute particles and elements much smaller than the flowing liquid of water or cloud or smoke—for it surpasses these far in quickness, and moves if touched by a more delicate cause, inasmuch as it is moved by images of smoke and mist, as for example when sunk in sleep we perceive altars exhale their steam on high and send up smoke (for without doubt these are images borne to us)—now, therefore, since, when vessels are shattered, you perceive the water flowing out on all sides and the liquid dispersing, and since mist and smoke disperse abroad into the air, believe that the spirit also is spread abroad and passes away far more quickly, and is more speedily dissolved into its first bodies, as soon as it has departed withdrawn from the limbs of man. In fact if the body, which is in a way its vessel, cannot contain it, when once broken up by any cause and rarified by the withdrawal of blood from the veins, how could you believe that it could be contained by any air, which is a more porous container than our body?

Besides, we feel that the mind is begotten along with the body, and grows up with it, and with it grows old. For as toddling children have a body infirm and tender, so a weak intelligence goes with it. Next, when their age has grown up into robust strength, the understanding too and the power of the mind is enlarged. Afterwards, when the body is now wrecked with the mighty strength of time, and the frame has succumbed with blunted strength, the intellect limps, the tongue babbles, the intelligence totters, all is wanting and fails at the same time. It follows therefore that the whole nature of the spirit is dissolved abroad, like smoke, into the high winds of the air, since we see it begotten along with the body, and growing up along with it, and as I have shown, falling to pieces at the same time worn out with age.

Add to this that, just as the body itself is liable to awful diseases and harsh pain, so we see the mind liable to carking care and grief and fear; therefore it follows that the mind also partakes of death.

Death, then, in Lucretius' view, is a severing of the mortal soul from the mortal body and leads to the dissolution of both into their constituent elements or atoms. There is nothing left of the individual and certainly no ascent to a home in the heavens. For Lucretius, as the following passage shows (*De rerum natura* III.830–842, tr. by W. H. D. Rouse and M. F. Smith), "death is nothing to us" (**Nīl igitur mors est ad nōs. . . .**):

Therefore death is nothing to us, it matters not one jot, since the nature of the mind is understood to be mortal; and as in time past we felt no distress, while from all quarters the Carthaginians were coming to the conflict, when the whole world, shaken by the terrifying tumult of war, shivered and quaked under the lofty and breezy heaven, and was in doubt under which domination all men were destined to fall by land and sea; so, when we shall no longer be, when the parting shall have come about between body and spirit from which we are compacted into one whole, then sure enough nothing at all will be able to happen to us, who will then no longer be, or to make us feel, not if earth be commingled with sea and sea with sky.

Lucretius also differs from Cicero in his views on the universe. In the view of the world contained in the "Somnium" everything above the moon is eternal, unchanging, and divine, the sphere of the fixed stars is the **summus deus**, and the sun is the **mēns mundī**. For Lucretius, all is perishable; nature, and not the gods, controls the universe; mind and intelligence can exist only in the human body as we know it, and the gods do not exist in any part of the world or universe that we can perceive but rather in abodes of a totally different order. These ideas, which are all diametrically opposed to those presented in the "Somnium," are set forth in the following extracts from Book V of the *De rerum natura* (V.64–69, 76–90, 126–145, and 146–154, tr. by W. H. D. Rouse and M. F. Smith):

> Now for what remains the order of my design has brought me to this point, that I must show how the frame of which the world consists is subject to death and has also had birth; in what ways that assemblage of matter established earth, sky, sea, and stars, the sun and the ball of the moon. . . .

> Besides, I will explain by what force pilot nature steers the courses of the sun and the goings of the moon; lest by any chance we think that these between heaven and earth traverse their yearly courses free, of their own will, and obliging for the increase of crops and of animals, or deem them to revolve by some plan of the gods. For if those who have been rightly taught that the gods lead a life without care, yet wonder all the while how things can go on, especially those transactions which are perceived overhead in the regions of ether, they revert back again to the old superstitions, and take to themselves cruel taskmasters, whom the poor wretches believe to be almighty, not knowing what can be and what cannot, in a word how each thing has limited power and a deep-set boundary mark. . . .

> For in fact it is not possible that the mind and understanding can be thought able to reside in any and every body; just as in the upper air there can be no tree, no clouds in the salt sea, as fish cannot live on the fields, blood cannot be in wood, nor sap in stones. It is fixed and ordained where each thing can grow and abide. So the mind cannot arise alone without a body, nor can it be far distant from sinews and blood. But if it could do this, the force of the mind itself could much more easily be in head or shoulders or down in the heels, and be born in any part, and at least abide in the same man, the same vessel. But since even in our own body there is seen to be a fixed rule and ordinance in what place spirit and mind can be and grow apart, so much the more must we deny that it can abide wholly outside the body and the animal structure in crumbling clods of earth or the sun's fire or in water or the lofty regions of air. Therefore these are not endowed with divine feeling, since they cannot be animated with life. . . .

> Another thing it is impossible that you should believe is that any holy abode of the gods exists in any part of the world. For the nature of the gods, being thin and far removed from our senses, is hardly seen by the mind's intelligence; and since it eludes the touch and impact of the hands, it cannot possibly touch anything that we can touch; for that cannot touch which may not be touched itself. Therefore their abodes also must be different from our abodes, being thin in accord with their bodies. . . .

MANILIUS, *ASTRONOMICA*

Marcus Manilius, who wrote a didactic epic poem on what we would call astrology in the early first century A.D. under the emperors Augustus and Tiberius, argues eloquently against the Epicurean view of the universe set forth by Lucretius and insists as does Cicero on the divinity of the heavens and the existence of a god or divine power that controls them. The following passages (*Astronomica* I.483–500 and 515–531, tr. G. P. Goold), though ostensibly arguing against Epicurus, could be thought of as a reply to the passages quoted above from Lucretius:

> For my part I find no argument so compelling as this to show that the universe moves in obedience to a divine power and is indeed the manifestation of God, and did not come together at the dictation of chance. Yet this is what he would have us believe who first built the walls of the heavens from minute atoms and into these resolved them again; he held that from these atoms are formed the seas, the lands, and the stars in the sky, and the air by which in its vast space worlds are created and dissolved; and that all matter returns to its first origins and changes the shape of things. Who could believe that such massive structures have been created from tiny atoms without the operation of a divine will, and that the universe is the creature of a blind compact? If chance gave such a world to us, chance itself would govern it. Then why do we see the stars arise in regular succession and duly perform as at the word of command their appointed courses, none hurrying ahead, none left behind? Why are the summer nights and the nights of winter ever made beautiful with the selfsame stars? Why does each day of the year bring back to the sky a fixed pattern and a fixed pattern leave at its departure?

> Everything born to a mortal existence is subject to change, nor does the earth notice that, despoiled by the passing years, it bears an appearance which varies through the ages. The firmament, however, conserving all its parts, remains intact, neither increased with length of time nor diminished by old age; it is neither the least bit warped by its motion nor wearied by its speed: it will remain the same for ever, since the same has it always been. No different heaven did our fathers see, no different heaven will our posterity behold. It is God, and changes not in time. That the Sun never deviates to the crosswise-lying Bears and never changes direction, setting course for the orient and bringing forth a dawn born of unwonted lands; that the Moon does not exceed her appointed orbs of light, but preserves the regularity of her waxing and waning; that the stars poised in heaven fall not upon Earth but take fixed periods of time to accomplish their orbits: all this is not the result of chance, but the plan of a God most high.

SENECA

Lucius Annaeus Seneca, born in Cordoba, Spain, sometime between 4 B.C. and A.D. 1, went to Rome, where he studied rhetoric and philosophy. He tutored the young Nero and then served as his adviser when he became emperor. In the early years of Nero's reign, Seneca and Burrus, the prefect of the pretorian guard, were able to moderate Nero's tendencies to excessive and violent actions. When the situation became intolerable, Seneca retired from his life at the court. He was ordered by Nero to commit suicide in A.D. 65 because of suspicion that he was implicated in the Pisonian conspiracy to overthrow the emperor.

Seneca wrote moral essays and letters, and he wrote tragedies on Greek mythological themes. In both his moral works and his tragedies he was much concerned with death and the possibility of an afterlife. His philosophical position leaned toward that of the Stoics, but he maintained an eclecticism that allowed him to express upon occasion views like those of the Epicureans. In the first passage below, the chorus in the *Troades*, the tragedy on the fall of Troy, sings a lyrical song in which it speculates in language reminiscent of Lucretius that the soul disperses at death and that there is no afterlife (371–408, tr. by F. J. Miller):

> Is it true, or does the tale cheat timid souls, that spirits live on when bodies have been buried, when the wife has closed her husband's eyes, when the last day has blotted out the sun, when the mournful urn holds fast our dust? Profits it not to give up the soul to death, but remains it for wretched mortals to live still longer? Or do we wholly die and does no part of us remain, when with the fleeting breath the spirit, mingling with vapours, has passed into the air, and the lighted fire has touched the naked body?
>
> All that the rising sun and all that the setting knows, all that the ocean laves with its blue waters, twice ebbing and twice flowing, time with the pace of Pegasus shall gather in. With such whirlwind speed as the twelve signs fly along, with such swift course as the lord of stars hurries on the centuries, and in such wise as Hecate hastens along her slanting ways, so do we all seek fate, and nevermore does he exist at all who has reached the pool whereby the high gods swear. As smoke from burning fires vanishes, staining the air for one brief moment; as clouds, which but now we saw lowering, are scattered by the cold blasts of Boreas, so shall this spirit which rules our bodies flow away. There is nothing after death, and death itself is nothing, the final goal of a course full swiftly run. Let the eager give up their hopes; their fears, the anxious; greedy time and chaos engulf us altogether. Death is a something that admits no cleavage, destructive to the body and unsparing of the soul. Taenarus and the cruel tyrant's kingdom and Cerberus, guarding the portal of no easy passage—all are but idle rumors, empty words, a tale light as a troubled dream. Dost ask where thou shalt lie when death has claimed thee? Where they lie who were never born.

One of Seneca's moral essays was written to console a woman named Marcia for the death of a son. In one passage of this essay he seeks to console the bereaved woman by assuring her in terms reminiscent of the choral ode from the *Troades* above and of Lucretius that death brings no ills and is in fact nothing (**nihil est**). This translation of *Ad Marciam* XIX.4–5 is by J. W. Basore:

Reflect that there are no ills to be suffered after death, that the reports that make the Lower World terrible to us are mere tales, that no darkness is in store for the dead, no prison, no blazing streams of fire, no river of Lethe, that no judgement-seats are there, nor culprits, nor in that freedom so unfettered are there a second time any tyrants. All these things are the fancies of the poets, who have harrowed us with groundless terrors. Death is a release from all suffering, a boundary beyond which our ills cannot pass—it restores us to that peaceful state in which we lay before we were born. If anyone pities the dead, he must also pity those who have not been born. Death is neither a good nor an evil; for that only which is something is able to be a good or an evil. But that which is itself nothing and reduces all things to nothingness consigns us to neither sphere of fortune: for evils and goods must operate upon something material.

Later in this same essay Seneca takes a very different tack and attempts to console Marcia by assuring her that the soul of her son has survived death and ascended to a place in the heavens which is very reminiscent of the setting of Scipio's dream in Cicero. The entire passage repays careful comparison with the "Somnium Scipionis." It is remarkable that within this single consolatory essay Seneca should express such very different views of death. It is as if he were unable to decide between the views of the soul expressed by Cicero and those expressed by Lucretius and so simply set them both side by side in the same essay. The translation is again that of J. W. Basore (*Ad Marciam* XXIV.5–XXV.2):

Only the image of your son—and a very imperfect likeness it was— has perished; he himself is eternal and has reached now a far better state, stripped of all outward encumbrances and left simply himself. This vesture of the body which we see, bones and sinews and the skin that covers us, this face and the hands that serve us and the rest of our human wrapping—these are but chains and darkness to our souls. By these things the soul is crushed and strangled and stained and, imprisoned in error, is kept far from its true and natural sphere. It constantly struggles against this weight of flesh in the effort to avoid being dragged back and sunk; it ever strives to rise to that place from which it once descended. There eternal peace awaits it when it has passed from earth's dull motley to the vision of all that is pure and bright.

There is no need, therefore, for you to hurry to the tomb of your son; what lies there is his basest part and a part that in life was the source of much trouble—bones and ashes are no more a part of him than were his clothes and the other protections of his body. He is complete—leaving nothing of himself behind, he has fled away and wholly departed from earth; for a little while he tarried above us while he was being purified and was ridding himself of all the blemishes and stain that still clung to him from his mortal existence, then soared aloft and sped away to join the souls of the blessed. A saintly band gave him welcome—the Scipios and the Catos and, joined with those who scorned life and through a draught of poison found freedom, your father, Marcia. Although there all are akin with all, he keeps his grandson near him, and, while your son rejoices in the newfound light, he instructs him in the movement of the neighboring stars, and gladly initiates him into Nature's secrets, not by guesswork, but by experience having true knowledge of them all; and just as a stranger is grateful for a guide through an unknown city, so your son, as he searches into the causes of celestial things, is grateful for a kinsman as his instructor. He bids him also turn his gaze upon the things of earth far below; for it is a pleasure to look back upon all that has been left behind.

EXERCISES

Exercise I: Verbs

Using the English cues in parentheses as guides, give the correct Latin verb forms (all subjunctives) to fill the blanks in the following sentences. Then give the name of the subjunctive construction used in each sentence.

EXAMPLE: Cum in Āfricam _____*vēnissem*_____ , nihil mihi fuit potius quam ut Massinissam convenīrem. (I had come) *circumstantial* **cum** *clause*

1. Quaesīvī tamen _____ ipse et Paulus pater. (whether . . . was alive)
2. Hominēs enim sunt hāc lēge generātī, quī _____ illum globum. (watch over—**tuērī**)
3. Mēns mundī est Sōl, tantā magnitūdine ut cūncta suā lūce _____ et _____ . (surveys—**lūstrāre**) (fills—**complēre**)
4. Apud eōs est nēmō quī ūnīus annī memōriam cōnsequī _____ . (can)
5. Quid dē tē aliī loquantur, ipsī _____ . (let them see to it)
6. Cum ad multam noctem _____ , artior quam solēbat somnus mē complexus est. (I had stayed awake—**vigilāre**)
7. Vōbīs retinendus animus est nē mūnus deōrum dēfūgisse _____ . (you seem)
8. Cum pateat igitur aeternum id esse quod ā sē ipsō _____ , quis est quī hanc nātūram animīs esse tribūtam _____ ? (is moved) (would deny)
9. Hic vērō tantus est tōtīus mundī incitātissimā conversiōne sonitus ut eum aurēs hominum capere nōn _____ . (can)

Exercise II: Dative or Ablative Case?

Translate the following with special attention to the italicized words. Then for each example identify the case of the italicized word or words and give the reason for the case. Select from the reasons given at the end of the exercise; some may be used more than once.

EXAMPLE: coetūs hominum *iūre* sociātī
          gatherings of men allied by law
          ablative of means

1. erit cognōmen id *tibi*
2. ostendās *patriae* lūmen animī tuī
3. ubi beātī *aevō sempiternō* fruantur
4. nihil acceptius est *illī deō*
5. perterritus eram *metū*

6. deus *istīs* tē *custōdiīs* līberāverit
7. hominēs *hāc lēge* generātī sunt
8. stellae orbēs cōnficiunt *celeritāte mīrābilī*
9. animus *vōbīs* retinendus est
10. omnia *mihi contemplantī* praeclāra vidēbantur
11. lūna *lūce* lūcēbat *aliēnā*
12. hominum *generī* prosperus est Iuppiter
13. in tellūrem feruntur omnia *nūtū suō* pondera
14. nec *silentiō* tantī mōtūs incitārī possunt
15. aperuērunt *sibi* reditum in hunc locum
16. ea gēns *sēnsū* audiendī caret
17. sōlis *ardōre* torrētur cingulum medium
18. ēluviōnēs *tempore certō* accidunt
19. hominēs annum sōlis *reditū* mētiuntur
20. *decorī vestrō* nōn dēfuī

ablative of cause	ablative with special verbs
ablative of manner	dative with adjective
ablative of means	dative of agent
ablative of separation	dative with compound verb
ablative of specification	dative indirect object
ablative of time when	dative of possession

Exercise III: Grammatical Forms

Match the names of the forms in the first column with the examples in the second:

1. _____ gerundive
2. _____ supine
3. _____ comparative adverb
4. _____ syncopated verb form
5. _____ superlative adverb
6. _____ present participle
7. _____ imperative
8. _____ perfect passive participle
9. _____ infinitive
10. _____ impersonal verb

A. interiectās
B. vigilāssem
C. cubitum
D. paenitet
E. ōcius
F. migrandum
G. contemplantī
H. extinctōs esse
I. scītō
J. sanctissimē

Exercise IV: Pronouns and Adjectives

Read the following selection. Then give the requested information for each word from the passage in the list below it. In identifying the type of pronoun or adjective, use the terms given under the list.

"Ex *hīs ipsīs* cultīs nōtīsque terrīs num aut tuum aut *cuiusquam nostrum* nōmen vel Caucasum *hunc, quem* cernis, trānscendere potuit vel *illum* Gangēn trānatāre? *Quis* in reliquīs orientis aut obeuntis sōlis ultimīs aut aquilōnis austrīve partibus tuum nōmen audiet? *Quibus* amputātīs cernis profectō *quantīs* in angustiīs vestra sē glōria dīlatārī velit. *Ipsī* autem, *quī* dē *nōbīs* loquuntur, quam loquentur diū?

	TYPE OF PRONOUN OR ADJECTIVE	CASE	NUMBER	MEANING
EXAMPLE: hīs	demonstrative	ablative	plural	these
1. ipsīs				
2. cuiusquam				
3. nostrum				
4. hunc				
5. quem				
6. illum				
7. Quis				
8. Quibus				
9. quantīs				
10. sē				
11. Ipsī				
12. quī				
13. nōbīs				

demonstrative, indefinite, intensive, interrogative, linking **quī**, personal, reflexive, relative

Exercise V: Translation into Latin

Translate the following group of statements into one Latin sentence. Your translation of the underlined words will help you organize the parts into one connected whole.

For human beings were generated (**generō**, 1) according to this law: they are to protect this planet (**globus**), the one you see in the middle region of the universe (**in hōc templō medium**). It is called earth. And to them has been given a soul from those eternal flames. These (*neuter plural*) you call the constellations (**sīdus**) and stars. These are global in shape (**globōsus**) and round (**rotundus**), animated (**animō**, 1) by divine minds. And (**-que**) they complete their circles and orbits with marvelous swiftness.

Exercise VI: Principal Parts

Give the missing principal parts, and then give the meaning of each verb.

EXAMPLE:

referō	referre	*rettulī*	relātum	*to bring back*
1. pateō				
2. _____	nancīscī			
3. _____	_____	caruī		
4. _____	_____	_____	attactum	
5. _____	_____	_____		to be able
6. pariō				
7. _____	dīlātāre			
8. _____	_____	māluī		
9. _____	_____	nīxus sum		
10. _____	_____	_____		to arise
11. praebeō				
12. _____	percontārī			

VOCABULARY

A

ā, ab (+ *abl.*), from, by
absēns, -ntis, absent, in one's absence
ac, and
accidō, -ere (3), **-ī**, to happen
accipiō, -ipere (3), **-ēpī, -eptum**, to receive, accept, entertain
*****acūtus, -a, -um**, sharp, pointed, (of sounds) high-pitched
ad (+ *acc.*), to, toward, for
adferō, -rre (*irreg.*), **attulī, allātum**, to bring
aditus, -ūs (*m*), approach, access
adsum, -esse (*irreg.*), **-fuī, -futūrus**, to be present
*****adversus, -a, -um**, turned to or toward a thing, standing over against, opposite
Aegyptus, -ī (*m*), Egypt
aetās, -ātis (*f*), age, time of life
*****aeternus, -a, -um**, everlasting, eternal
Āfricānus, -ī (*m*), Publius Cornelius Scipio Africanus Major
*****agitō** (1), to put a thing in motion, drive, impel, move
agō, agere (3), **ēgī, āctum**, to do, act, drive, treat, give (thanks), celebrate (a triumph)
alacer, -cris, -cre, eager, brisk, active
aliēnus, -a, -um, foreign
aliquis, aliquid, someone, anyone, something, anything
*****aliunde**, from another place, person, or thing
alius, -a, -ud, other
  aliī . . . aliī, some . . . others
alter, -ra, -rum, the one, the other (of two)
altus, -a, -um, high
amīcus, -a, -um, friendly
*****angustiae, -ārum** (*f pl*), narrowness, shortness, want, difficulty
angustus, -a, -um, narrow
animus, -ī (*m*) mind, soul, courage
annus, -ī (*m*), year
ante (*adv.*), before
aperiō, -īre (4), **-uī, -tum**, to open
appellō (1), to name, call
apud (+ *acc.*), among
*****aquilō, -ōnis** (*m*) north wind, north
arbitror, -ārī (1), **-ātus sum**, to think
Asia, -ae (*f*), Asia (Minor)
*****aspiciō, -icere** (3), **-exī, -ectum**, to look at, see

*****astrum, -ī** (*n*), star, constellation, heavenly body, the sun
atque, and
attingō, -tingere (3), **-tigī, -tactum**, to touch, reach
audeō, -dēre (2), **-sus sum**, to dare
audiō (4), to hear
augeō, -ēre (2), **-xī, -ctum**, to increase
*****auris, -is** (*f*), ear
aut, or
  aut . . . aut, either . . . or
autem, moreover, however, but, and in fact, indeed

B

bellum, -ī (*n*), war
bene, well
bonus, -a, -um, good

C

*****caelum, -ī** (*n*), sky, heavens
capiō, -ere (3), **cēpī, -tum**, to take, capture, perceive
Capitōlium, -ī (*n*), the Capitoline Hill in Rome
causa, -ae (*f*), cause, reason
celeritās, -ātis (*f*), speed, swiftness
cernō, -ere (3), **crēvī, crētum**, to see
certus, -a, -um, fixed, certain, sure
cēterī, -ae, -a, the rest (of), the other, others
circum (+ *acc.*), around
circumdō, -are (1), **-edī, -atum**, to surround
cīvitās, -ātis (*f*), state
coepī, -isse, -tum, to have begun
*****coetus, -ūs** (*m*), a coming or meeting together, assembling, uniting
cōgitō (1), to think
cōgō, -ere (3), **coēgī, coāctum**, to compel
*****colō, -ere** (3), **-uī, cultum**, to cultivate, tend, care for, practice, devote oneself to
*****complector, -ctī** (3), **-xus sum**, to embrace
*****compleō, -ēre** (2), **-ēvī, -ētum**, to fill up
concilium, -ī (*n*), council, meeting
cōnficiō, -icere (3), **-ēcī, -ectum**, to accomplish, finish, make
conlacrimō (1), to weep very much

cōnsequor, -quī (3), **-cūtus sum**, to follow, attain
cōnsilium, -ī (*n*), plan, counsel
cōnsistō, -sistere (3), **-stitī**, to stand, stop, halt
cōnspiciō, -icere (3), **-exī, -ectum**, to see, catch sight of
cōnstituō, -uere (3), **-uī, -ūtum**, to set up, put in order
cōnsul, -lis (*m*), consul
cōnsūmō, -ere (3), **-psī, -ptum**, to consume, use up
contemnō, -nere (3), **-psī, -ptum**, to despise, scorn
*__contemplō__ (1), to survey, behold, observe, consider
contineō, -inēre (2), **-inuī, -entum**, to hold together, constrain
*__conversiō, -ōnis__ (*f*), a turning around, revolving, revolution
*__convertō, -tere__ (3), **-tī, -sum**, to turn back, turn, whirl around, complete (a period of time) in the course of a revolution, (passive in reflexive sense) revolve
corpus, -oris (*n*), body
crēdō, -ere (3), **-idī, -itum**, to believe
cum (+ *abl.*), with
cum, when, since
*__cūnctus, -a, -um__, all
cupiō, -ere (3), **-īvī** or **-iī, -ītum**, to desire
cūra, -ae (*f*), care, concern
cursus, -ūs (*m*), running, course
*__custōdia, -ae__ (*f*), guard, protection, custody, confinement, prison

D

de (+ *abl.*), from, down from, concerning, about, for
dēclārō (1), to make known, reveal, declare
*__decus, -oris__ (*n*), splendor, glory, honor
dēdō, -ere (3), **-idī, -itum**, to surrender, give up
*__dēficiō, -ere__ (3), **-ēcī, -ectum**, to loosen, set free, desert, fail, (of the sun or moon) suffer eclipse
deinde, then, next
dēleō, -ēre (2), **-ēvī, -ētum**, to destroy
dēligō, -igere (3), **-ēgī, -ēctum**, to choose, select
dēmōnstrō (1), to show, point out
dēserō, -ere (3), **-uī, -tum**, to abandon, desert
dēspērō (1), to despair of
dēsum, -esse (*irreg.*), **-fuī, -futūrus** (+ *dat.*), to fail, be lacking
deus, -ī (*m*), god
   dī, plural of **deus**
dīcō, -cere (3), **-xī, -ctum**, to say, call
dictātor, -ōris (*m*), dictator
diēs, -ēī (*m/f*), day
*__discēdō, -dere__ (3), **-ssī, -ssum**, to go away, depart
*__distinctus, -a, -um__, separate, distinct
diū, a long time

dīvīnus, -a, -um, divine
dō, dare (1), **dedī, datum**, to give
domus, -ūs (*f*), house, home
duo, duae, duo, two
dux, -cis (*m*), leader

E

ē, ex (+ *abl.*), out of, from
efficiō, -icere (3), **-ēcī, -ectum**, to cause, effect, bring about
ego, I
enim, for, indeed
*__equidem__, indeed
et, and
etiam, also, even
etsī, although
ex, ē (+ *abl.*), out of, from
exerceō (2), to train, exercise
exiguus, -a, -um, small, scanty
expectō (1), to hope for
expōnō, -ōnere (3), **-osuī, -ositum**, to explain, set forth
*__extinguō, -guere__ (3), **-xī, -ctum**, to put out, extinguish, kill, destroy, annihilate
extrā, outside, beyond
extrēmus, -a, -um, outermost, last

F

facile, easily
faciō, -ere (3), **fēcī, factum**, to make, do
familia, -ae (*f*), family
fāta, -ōrum (*n pl*), the fates
fātālis, -is, -e, ordained, allotted by fate
ferē, almost, approximately, usually
ferō, -rre (*irreg.*), **tulī, lātum**, to bring, carry
figūra, -ae (*f*), form, shape, figure
fīnis, -is (*m*), end
fīō, fierī (*irreg.*), **factus sum**, to be done, happen
flamma, -ae (*f*), flame
fleō, -ēre (2), **-ēvī, -ētum**, to weep
fōrma, -ae (*f*), shape, appearance
futūrus, -a, -um, about to be, future

G

gēns, -tis (*f*), tribe
genus, -eris (*n*), kind, class, race
globōsus, -a, -um, spherical
*__globus, -ī__ (*m*) round body, sphere, globe
glōria, -ae (*f*), fame, glory
Graecia, -ae (*f*), Greece
gravis, -is, -e, heavy, (of sound) low-pitched

H

habeō (2), to have, hold, consider
   *__habētō__ = future imperative of **habeō**, "reckon," "consider"
habitābilis, -is, -e, habitable
habitō (1), to inhabit

hīc (*adv.*), here, at this point
hic, haec, hoc, this
Homērus, -ī (*m*), Homer, ancient Greek epic poet, author of the *Iliad* and the *Odyssey*
homō, -inis (*m*), man, human being
hūc, to this place
hūmānus, -a, -um, human

I

iam, already, now
īdem, eadem, idem, the same
igitur, therefore
ignis, -is (*m*), fire
*iīs = eīs
ille, illa, illud, that, he, she, it
imperium, -ī (*n*), command, power, empire
in (+ *abl.*), in
in (+ *acc.*), into, toward
incitō (1), to set in motion
incolō, -ere (3), **-uī**, to inhabit, dwell in
*īnfimus, -a, -um, lowest
inquam, to say
īnsidiae, -ārum (*f pl*), ambush, plot
īnsula, -ae (*f*), island
inter (+ *acc.*), between, among
interest, -esse (*irreg.*), **-fuit** (*impersonal*), it makes a difference, matters
interior, -ius, inner
*intervallum, -ī (*n*), space between, interval, distance
*intueor, -ērī (2), **-itus sum**, to look at or toward, look to for help
ipse, ipsa, ipsum (*intensive*), -self
is, ea, id, this, that, he, she, it
iste, ista, istud, that (of yours)
ita, so, thus
itaque, and so, therefore
iterum, again
iūs, iūris (*n*), right, law
iūstus, -a, -um, just, right

K

Karthāgō, -inis (*f*), Carthage, city in North Africa

L

lacrima, -ae (*f*), tear
lātus, -a, -um, broad, wide
latus, -eris (*n*), side, flank
laus, -dis (*f*), praise
legiō, -ōnis (*f*), legion
lēx, lēgis (*f*), law
līberō (1), to free
locus, -ī (*m*), (*pl*) **loca, -ōrum** (*n*), place
longus, -a, -um, long
loquor, -ī (3), **locūtus sum**, to speak, talk
*lūmen, -inis (*n*), light
lūna, -ae (*f*), moon
lūx, lūcis (*f*), light

M

magis, more
magnitūdō, -inis (*f*), size
magnus, -a, -um, large, great
maneō, -ēre (2), **-sī, -sum**, to remain
manus, -ūs (*f*), hand
mare, -is (*n*), sea
maximē, especially
maximus, -a, -um, greatest, very great
medius, -a, -um, middle (of)
melior, melius, better
*meminī, -inisse, to remember, recall, mention
memoria, -ae (*f*), memory
mēns, -tis (*f*), mind
metus, -ūs (*m*), fear
meus, -a, -um, my, mine
*migrō (1), to depart
mīles, -itis (*m*), soldier
minimus, -a, -um, smallest
*mīrābilis, -is, -e, wonderful, marvelous, extraordinary
modo, only
mōns, -tis (*m*), mountain
morior, -ī (3), **-tuus sum**, to die
moror, -ārī (1), **-ātus sum**, to delay
mors, -tis (*f*), death
*mortālis, -is, -e, subject to death, mortal
mōtus, -ūs (*m*), movement
moveō, -ēre (2), **mōvī, mōtum**, to move
multus, -a, -um, much, (pl.) many
*mundus, -ī (*m*), the earth, world, universe
mūnus, -eris (*n*), gift

N

nam, for
namque, for indeed, for
nancīscor, -ī (3), **nactus sum**, to find, obtain
nāscor, -ī (3), **nātus sum**, to be born
nātūra, -ae (*f*), nature
nātūrālis, -is, -e, natural
nē . . . quidem, not even
-ne: indicates a question
nē, that . . . not, lest, don't
nec, and . . . not
   nec (neque) . . . nec, neither . . . nor
necesse (*indeclinable*), necessary
negō (1), to say . . . not, deny
nēmō, no one
neque, neither
   neque . . . neque (nec), neither . . . nor
nihil (*n*), nothing
Nīlus, -ī (*m*), Nile
nisi, except, unless, if . . . not
nōmen, -inis (*n*), name
nōminō (1), to name
nōn, not
nōndum, not yet
Nōnne . . . ? (introduces a question that expects the answer "yes")
nōnus, -a, -um, ninth

73

nōs, we, us
noster, -tra, -trum, our
*****nōtus, -a, -um**, known
novem, nine
nox, -ctis (*f*), night
nūllus, -a, -um, no, none
Num . . . ? Surely . . . not . . . ? (introduces a question that expects the answer "no")
numerus, -ī (*m*), number
numquam, never
nunc, now

O

ob (+ *acc.*), on account of
obtineō, -inēre (2), **-inuī, -entum**, to hold, occupy
octō, eight
oculus, -ī (*m*), eye
omnis, -is, -e, all, every
oportet, -ēre (2), **-tuit** (*impersonal*), it behooves, one ought
oppugnō (1), to attack, storm
optimus, -a, -um, best
*****orbis, -is** (*m*), circle, orbit
orior, -īrī (4), **-tus sum**, to rise, arise
ostendō, -dere (3), **-dī, -tum**, to show

P

paene, almost
parēns, -ntis (*m/f*), parent
pareō, -ēre (2), **-uī, -itum** (+ *dat.*), to obey
*****pariō, -ere** (3) **peperī, -tum**, to bring forth, give birth to, bring about, produce
pars, -tis (*f*), part
parvus, -a, -um, small
pateō, -ēre (2), **-uī**, to extend, be open, stand open, be evident
pater, -tris (*m*), father
patria, -ae (*f*), fatherland
paucī, -ae, -a, few
per (+ *acc.*), through, by
perterritus, -a, -um, terrified
pertineō, -ēre (2), **-uī**, to extend
*****plēnus, -a, -um** (+ *gen.*), full (of)
pōnō, pōnere (3), **posuī, positum**, to put, place
populus, -ī (*m*), people, nation
possum, posse (*irreg.*), **potuī**, to be able, can
*****post** (*adv.*), afterward
posteā (*adv.*), afterward
posterī, -ōrum (*m pl*), descendants, future generations
praebeō (2), to furnish, offer
praemium, -ī (*n*), reward
praesertim, especially
praeter (+ *acc.*), except
prīnceps, -ipis, chief, foremost
prīnceps, -ipis (*m*), chief
*****prīncipium, -ī** (*n*), beginning, first cause of motion
prō (+ *abl.*), according to

prōdō, -ere (3), **-idī, -itum**, to hand on
proficīscor, -icīscī (3), **-ectus sum**, to set out, start, depart
prohibeō (2), to restrain, stop from (+ infinitive)
propinquus, -ī (*m*), kinsman
propter (+ *acc.*), on account of
prōvideō, -idēre (2), **-īdī, -īsum**, to see into the future, plan ahead
pūblicus, -a, -um, public

Q

quaerō, -rere (3), **-sīvī** or **-siī, -sītum**, to ask
*****quaesō, -ere** (3), to beg, pray, beseech
quam, how, as, than, as . . . as possible
   quam maximē, as much as possible
quandō, when
quantus, -a, -um, how great, how much
quārtus, -a, -um, fourth
*****quasi**, as if, as it were
-que, and
quī, quae, quod, who, which, that
quia, because
quīdam, quaedam, quiddam (or **quoddam**), (a) certain (one)
quidem, indeed, certainly, at least
*****quīn**, but that, that, from, why don't? why not?
*****quīn etiam**, but, indeed, really, nay even
quis, quid, who? what? why?
quisquam, quicquam (or **quidquam**), anyone, anything, (adjective) any
quisque, quaeque, quidque (or **quodque**), each, each one
quod, because
quoniam, since

R

*****radius, -ī** (*m*), beam, ray
ratiō, -ōnis (*f*), reason
redeō, -īre (*irreg.*), **-īvī** or **-iī, -itum**, to return, go back
*****reditus, -ūs** (*m*), return, returning
*****referō, -rre** (*irreg.*), **rettulī, relātum**, to bring back, return
regiō, -ōnis (*f*), region
rēgius, -a, -um, royal
rēgnum, -ī (*n*), kingdom
regō, -gere (3), **-xī, -ctum**, to rule
reliquus, -a, -um, remaining, the rest of
rēs, reī (*f*), thing, matter, affair
rēs pūblica, reī pūblicae (*f*), state, republic
revertor, -tī (3), **-sus sum**, to return, go back
rēx, rēgis (*m*), king
Rōmānus, -a, -um, Roman
Rōmulus, -ī (*m*), the founder of Rome
rotundus, -a, -um, round, circular, spherical

S

*****saeculum, -ī** (*n*), race, breed, generation,

lifetime, age, the longest lifetime of a man, period of a hundred years, century
saepe, often
salūs, -ūtis (*f*), safety
sciō, (4), to know
****scītō** = future imperative of **sciō**
scrībō, -bere (3), **-psī, -ptum**, to write
sē, himself, itself, themselves
sed, but
****sēdēs, -is** (*f*), seat, dwelling place, location
semper, always
****sempiternus, -a, -um**, everlasting
senātus, -ūs (*m*), senate
senex, -is (*m*), old man
****sēnsus, -ūs** (*m*), perception, sensation, sense
sentiō, -īre (4), **-sī, -sum**, to feel, perceive, think
septem, seven
****sermō, -ōnis** (*m*), conversation
sēsē, itself
sī, if
sibi, to or for himself, herself, themselves
sīc, so, thus
sīcut, just as
silentium, -ī (*n*), silence
****sīquidem**, if indeed, if it is really true that
socius, -ī (*m*), ally
sōl, sōlis (*m*), sun
****soleō, -ēre** (2), **solitus sum**, to be accustomed
sōlus, -a, -um, only, alone
sōlum, only
somnus, -ī (*m*), sleep
****sonitus, -ūs** (*m*), sound
****sonus, -ī** (*m*), noise, sound
spectō (1), to look, look at
spēs, -eī (*f*), hope
****stella, -ae** (*f*), star
stō, stāre (1), **stetī, statum**, to stand
studium, -ī (*n*), study, pursuit
sum, esse (*irreg.*), **fuī, futūrus**, to be
summa, -ae (*f*), sum, sum total
summus, -a, -um, highest, greatest
suprā (+ *acc.*), above
suspicor, -ārī (1), **-ātus sum**, to suspect
suus, -a, -um, his (own), its (own), their (own)

T

tam, so much, so
tamen, nevertheless
tantus, -a, -um, so great, such a great
****templum, -ī** (*n*), an open space in the sky marked out by the augur with his staff for a religious observance as he watches for omens, any open space, the entire sky, a sacred place, temple
tempus, -oris (*n*), time
teneo, -ēre (2), **-uī, -tum**, to hold, keep
terra, -ae (*f*), earth, land

timor, -ōris (*m*), fear
tōtus, -a, -um, all, whole
trādō, -ere (3), **-idī, -itum** (+ *dat.*), to hand over, commit to, transmit, hand down
trahō, -here (3), **-xī, -ctum**, to drag, draw
tribūnus, -ī (*m*), tribune
tribuō, -uere (3), **-uī, -ūtum**, to assign, attribute
tū, you (sing.)
tueor, -ērī (2), **tuitus** (or **tūtus**) **sum**, to defend, guard
tum, then
tuus, -a, -um, your

U

ubi, when, where
ūllus, -a, -um, any
ultimus, -a, -um, farthest
umquam, ever
unde, from which place
ūnus, -a, -um, one, only, alone
urbs, urbis (*f*), city
ut, that, as, when
uterque, utraque, utrumque, both, each

V

vehemēns, -ntis, violent, severe
vel, or
  vel . . . vel, either . . . or
veniō, venīre (4), **vēnī, ventum**, to come
****vērō**, in truth, certainly, surely
****vertex, -icis** (*m*), whirlpool, coil of flame, highest point, summit, (pl.) poles of the heavens, projections of the earth's axis
vertō, -tere (3), **-tī, -sum**, to turn
vērus, -a, -um, true
vester, -tra, -trum, your
****vestīgium, -ī** (*n*), footstep, step
via, -ae (*f*), road, way
videō, vidēre (2), **vīdī, vīsum**, to see, (passive) seem
****vigilō** (1), to stay awake, be awake
vincō, -ere (3), **vīcī, victum**, to conquer, overcome, surpass
vir, virī (*m*), man
virtūs, -ūtis (*f*), manliness, resolution, courage
vīs, vim, vī (*f*), force, violence, flood, (pl.) strength
vīta, -ae (*f*), life
vīvō, -vere (3), **-xī, -ctum**, to live
vix, scarcely
vocō (1), to call
volō, velle (*irreg.*), **voluī**, to wish, be willing
****voluptās, -ātis** (*f*), satisfaction, enjoyment, pleasure, delight
vōs, you (pl.)
vulgus, -ī (*n*), the common people

CREDITS

TEXT CREDITS AND SOURCES

All of the following are reprinted by permission of the publishers and The Loeb Classical Library, Cambridge, Massachusetts: Harvard University Press, unless indicated otherwise.

Page 11: From *Sallust*, translated by J.C. Rolfe, © 1980; from *Cicero, Vol. XI*, translated by N.H. Watts, © 1979; from *Cicero, The Speeches*, translated by R. Gardner, © 1966. Pages 13–17: From *Velleius Paterculus*, translated by Frederick W. Shipley, © 1979. Page 17: From *Cicero, De Senectute, De Amicitia, De Divinatione*, translated by William Armistead Falconer, © 1964. © Oxford University Press 1967, reprinted from *Scipio Aemilianus* by A.E. Astin (1967) by permission of Oxford University Press. Page 19: From *Manilius, Astronomica*, translated by G.P. Goold, © 1977; from *Cicero, De Re Publica, De Legibus*, translated by Clinton Walker Keyes, © 1970. Page 21: From *Cicero, Letters to Atticus*, translated by E.O. Winstedt, © 1966. Page 23: From *Cicero, Vol. XIV*, translated by N.H. Watts, © 1979. Page 25: From *Cicero, De Natura Deorum, Academica*, translated by H. Rackham, © 1967. Page 27: From *Cicero, De Officiis*, translated by Walter Miller, © 1975. Pages 29, 31: From *Cicero De Natura Deorum, Academica*, translated by H. Rackham, © 1967. Page 33: From *The Institutio Oratoria of Quintilian*, translated by H.E. Butler, © 1980. Page 35: From *Aristotle, On the Heavens*, translated by W.K.C. Guthrie, © 1971. Pages 37, 39: From *Seneca, Naturales Quaestiones*, translated by Thomas H. Corcoran, © 1971. Page 41: From *Aristotle, Meteorologica*, translated by H.D.P. Lee, © 1962. Page 43: From *Seneca, Naturales Quaestiones*, translated by Thomas H. Corcoran, © 1971. Pages 43, 45, from *Cicero, De Natura Deorum, Academica*, translated by H. Rackham, © 1967. Page 49: From *Cicero, Tusculan Disputations*, translated by J.E. King, © 1966. Page 62: From *Lucretius, De Rerum Natura*, translated by W.H.D. Rouse and M.F. Smith, © 1975. Page 65: From *Manilius, Astronomica*, translated by G.P. Goold, © 1977. Page 66: From *Seneca, Tragedies*, translated by Frank Justus Miller, © 1979. Page 67: From *Seneca, Moral Essays*, translated by John W. Basore, © 1965.

PHOTO/ART CREDITS

Page 9: SCALA/Art Resource, NY. Page 18: Illustration by Claudia Karabaic Sargent. Page 20: Alinari/Art Resource, NY. Page 21: The J. Paul Getty Museum. Page 31: *Larousse Encyclopedia of Astronomy*, © 1959, Prometheus Press, New York. Page 34: Marburg/Art Resource, NY. Page 40: From *Manilius, Astronomica*, translated by G.P. Goold, © 1977. Reprinted by permission of the publishers and The Loeb Classical Library, Massachusetts: Harvard University Press. Page 42: The Bettmann Archive. Page 46: Biblioteca Apostolica Vaticana. Page 50: Alinari/Art Resource NY. Page 52: SCALA/Art Resource, NY. Page 53: Alinari/Art Resource, NY.